Classical Piano Anthology 2

25 Original Works
Including pieces by Haydn, Cimarosa, Beethoven
and Czerny

Selected and edited by Nils Franke

ED 13436
ISMN M-2201-3273-5
ISBN 978-1-84761-145-1

www.schott-music.com

Mainz • London • Berlin • Madrid • New York • Paris • Prague • Tokyo • Toronto
© 2011 SCHOTT MUSIC Ltd, London • Printed in Germany

Acknowledgements / Remerciements / Danksagung

I am grateful to Mary and David Bowerman whose generous support has enabled the CD to be recorded in the excellent setting of Champs Hill Music Room. A special mention must go to the production team of the CD, Ateş Orga and Ken Blair, for their expertise and contribution to this project.

Je remercie Mary et David Bowerman dont le généreux soutien a permis d'enregistrer le CD dans les excellentes conditions offertes par le Champs Hill Music Room. Il me faut également citer tout particulièrement l'équipe de production du CD, Ateş Orga et Ken Blair, pour leur savoir-faire et leur précieuse contribution à ce projet.

Ich danke Mary und David Bowerman für ihre großzügige Unterstützung, die es ermöglicht hat, die CD im großartigen Ambiente des Champs Hill Music Room aufzunehmen. Ein besonderer Dank geht an das Produktionsteam der CD, Ateş Orga und Ken Blair für ihr Know-how und ihren Beitrag zu diesem Projekt.

Nils Franke

ED 13436
British Library Cataloguing-in-Publication Data.
A catalogue record for this book is available from the British Library
ISMN M-2201-3273-5
ISBN 978-1-84761-145-1

CD recorded in Champs Hill, West Sussex, 26th April 2011, on a Steinway D Concert Grand with Nils Franke, Piano
Producer: Ateş Orga
Editor and Engineer: Ken Blair
Cover image: 'Die Insel Delos' (1847), by Carl Anton Joseph Rottmann

French translation: Michaëla Rubi
German translation: Heike Brühl
Music setting and page layout: Darius Heise-Krzyszton, www.notensatzstudio.de

Printed in Germany S&Co.8752

Contents / Sommaire / Inhalt Page / Seite

The Pieces / Les pièces / Die Stücke

Introduction

The present collection of piano pieces is the second volume in a series of four books covering the piano music in the classical period from grades 1–8. It follows on from a format established in the Romantic Piano Anthologies Vols. 1–4 (ED 12912 to ED 12915).

While anthologies are, inevitably, a personal selection of music they can nevertheless be underpinned by specific selection criteria. In the case of the present series, it has been my intention to include works that are idiomatically written, are indicative of their period and, above all, are useful in the development of pianistic skills for players at this stage of their development.

In the selection of repertoire I have tried to achieve a balance between established teaching pieces, rare works of the period, and between some of the main composers of the era and their lesser-known contemporaries. I hope that this can in some way attempt to reflect the diversity of styles within music from the 1760s to circa 1820.

The repertoire is presented broadly in an order of ascending difficulty, though I hope that the suggested sequence can be seen as a recommendation, rather than a restriction. The music included in this book is aimed at players of Grades 3–4 standard (UK) or lower intermediate to intermediate (USA), or pianists of four or more years' playing experience (Europe).

The teaching notes are designed to assist students by offering some suggestions on how to approach a particular section within a piece. Also included are suggestions for topics that may need to be considered when playing classical piano music on a modern instrument, as the fortepiano of the late eighteenth century was of a different construction to the modern piano. The commentary cannot, and is not intended to, replace the collaborative spirit of exploration that teachers and students share in their lessons.

One of the most rewarding aspects of instrumental teaching is watching students become independent learners who make their own decisions and develop their own performance skills. I hope that the Classical Piano Anthologies can in some way contribute to this development.

Nils Franke

Introduction

Ce recueil de pièces pour piano constitue le deuxième volet d'une collection en quatre volumes consacrés à la musique pour piano de la période classique, du niveau 1 au niveau 8. Du point de vue formel, il se calque sur le format établi dans l'Anthologie du piano romantique, volumes 1 à 4 (ED 12912 to ED 12915).

Le fait qu'une anthologie reflète inévitablement des choix personnels n'empêche pas qu'elle puisse néanmoins être sous-tendue pas des critères de sélection spécifiques. Pour ce qui concerne la présente collection, j'ai choisi d'inclure des œuvres à l'écriture idiomatique, caractéristiques de leur période et, avant tout, utiles au développement des compétences pianistiques des instrumentistes à ce niveau de leur progression.

Pour ce qui concerne le choix du répertoire, j'ai tenté de réaliser un équilibre aussi bien entre des pièces appartenant traditionnellement au répertoire pédagogique et des œuvres rares de cette période, qu'entre des compositeurs majeurs et leurs contemporains moins célèbres. J'espère que cela permettra d'illustrer en quelque sorte la diversité des styles musicaux des années 1760 à 1820 environ.

Le répertoire est présenté globalement par ordre croissant de difficulté, mais j'espère que la progression suggérée sera considérée davantage comme une suggestion que comme une contrainte. La musique proposée dans cet ouvrage s'adresse à des musiciens de niveau 3 à 4 standard (RU), intermédiaire à intermédiaire avancé (USA), ou à des pianistes possédant au moins quatre années de pratique instrumentale (Europe).

Les notes pédagogiques ont pour objectif d'aider les élèves en leur suggérant des axes de travail pour l'approche de certains passages spécifiques à l'intérieur des morceaux. Dans la mesure où le pianoforte de la fin du 18e siècle était de facture différente du piano moderne, elles proposent également des réflexions sur les thématiques à aborder lorsque l'on joue de la musique classique sur un instrument moderne. Ces commentaires ne peuvent ni ne prétendent se substituer à l'esprit de collaboration et d'exploration que partagent le maître et l'élève pendant la leçon.

L'un des aspects les plus gratifiants de l'enseignement instrumental est de voir ses élèves devenir indépendants, expérimenter différentes pistes musicales et développer leurs propres dons. J'espère qu'à leur manière, ces Anthologies du piano classique pourront contribuer à ce développement.

Nils Franke

Einleitung

Die vorliegende Sammlung mit Klavierstücken ist der zweite Band einer vierbändigen Reihe mit klassischer Klaviermusik für alle Schwierigkeitsgrade. Sie ist genauso aufgebaut wie die Romantic Piano Anthology Bd. 1–4 (ED 12912 bis ED 12915).

Eine Anthologie enthält zwar immer eine subjektive Auswahl von Musikstücken, doch können natürlich bestimmte Auswahlkriterien herangezogen werden. Mein Anliegen bei der Zusammenstellung der vorliegenden Reihe war eine Auswahl von Musikstücken, die idiomatisch geschrieben, typisch für ihre Epoche und vor allem im Hinblick auf klavierspielerische Aspekte für Pianisten der jeweiligen Spielstufe nützlich sind.

Bei der Auswahl der Stücke habe ich versucht, ein ausgewogenes Verhältnis zwischen bewährtem Unterrichtsmaterial und selten gespielten klassischen Werken sowie zwischen einigen der wichtigsten Komponisten dieser Epoche und ihren weniger bekannten Zeitgenossen herzustellen. Ich hoffe, dass dies die Stilvielfalt der Musik von ca. 1760 bis 1820 widerspiegelt.

Die Stücke sind weitgehend nach aufsteigendem Schwierigkeitsgrad geordnet, wobei die vorgeschlagene Reihenfolge als Empfehlung und nicht als Einschränkung aufgefasst werden sollte. Die Stücke in diesem Buch richten sich an Spieler der Stufe 3–4 (Großbritannien), untere Mittelstufe bzw. Mittelstufe (USA) bzw. Pianisten mit mindestens vier Jahren Spielpraxis (Europa).

Die Spielhinweise sollen die Schüler mit Hilfe von Vorschlägen für bestimmte Passagen an das jeweilige Stück heranführen. Darüber hinaus enthält die Anthologie Vorschläge, die eventuell berücksichtigt werden müssen, wenn man klassische Klaviermusik auf einem modernen Instrument spielt, da sich das Pianoforte des späten 18. Jahrhunderts vom modernen Klavier unterschied. Die Anmerkungen können und sollen jedoch nicht die gemeinsame Beschäftigung von Lehrern und Schülern mit dem Stück im Unterricht ersetzen.

Eine der schönsten Belohnungen beim Unterrichten eines Instruments ist, zu beobachten, wie die Schüler unabhängig werden, eigene Entscheidungen treffen und ihren eigenen Spielstil entwickeln. Ich hoffe, dass die Bände der Classical Piano Anthology einen Betrag zu dieser Entwicklung leisten können.

Nils Franke

1. Allegro

from Divertimento No. 2 WWV 43

Georg Christoph Wagenseil
(1715-1777)

Allegro (♩. = 66–72)

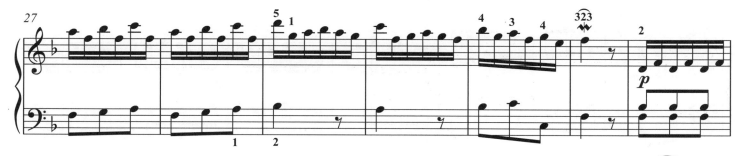

2. Sonata in G major

Domenico Cimarosa
(1749–1801)

Allegro (♩. = 60)

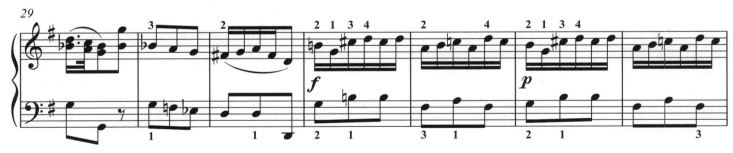

3. Rondo

from Sonatina Op. 12 No. 9

James Hook
(1746-1827)

Allegretto (♩ = 88)

Fine

D. C. al Fine

4. English Dance

No. 15

Carl Ditters von Dittersdorf
(1739–1799)

(♩ = 96)

Fine

D. C. al Fine

5. Guaracha

from Pianoforte Method

Johann Baptist Cramer
(1771–1858)

Allegro moderato *)
(♩. = 76)

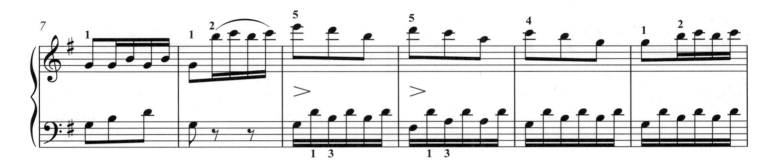

*) Fingering is the composer's own / Le doigté sont du compositeur / Der Fingersatz stammt von Komponisten

6. Vivace

from Sonatina Op. 12 No. 8

Samuel Wesley
(1766–1837)

7. Allegro

Johann Nepomuk Hummel
(1778–1837)

*) Fingering is the composer's own / Le doigté sont du compositeur / Der Fingersatz stammt von Komponisten

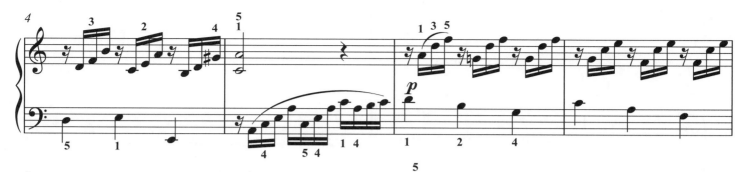

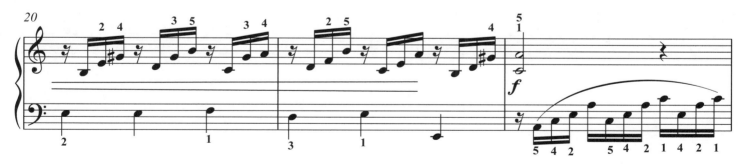

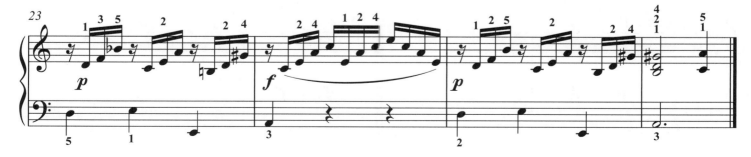

8. Ländler

D378 No. 3

Franz Schubert
(1797–1828)

9. Ländlerischer Tanz

WoO 11 No. 2

Ludwig van Beethoven
(1770–1827)

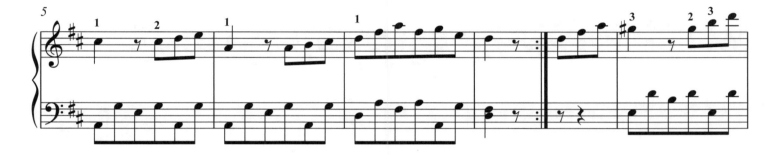

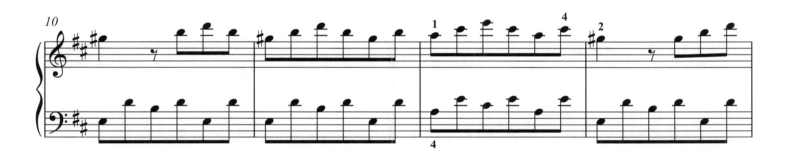

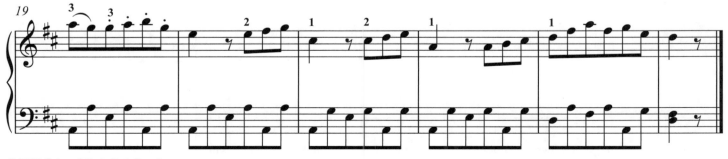

10. Praeludium and Andantino

from Pianoforte Method

Johann Baptist Cramer
(1771–1858)

*) Fingering is the composer's own / Le doigté sont du compositeur / Der Fingersatz stammt von Komponisten

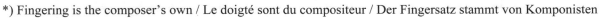

11. Allegro assai

Op. 38 No. 20

Johann Wilhelm Hässler
(1747–1822)

12. Presto

Op. 38 No. 29

Johann Wilhelm Hässler
(1747–1822)

13. Andante

Op. 453 No. 32

Carl Czerny
(1791–1857)

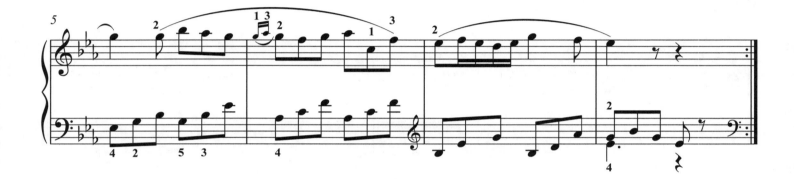

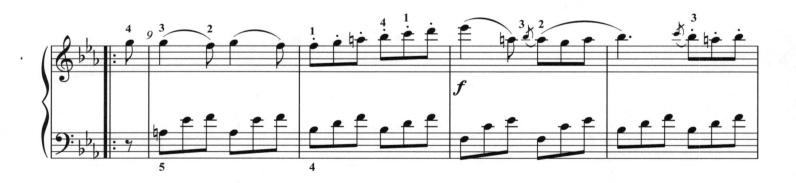

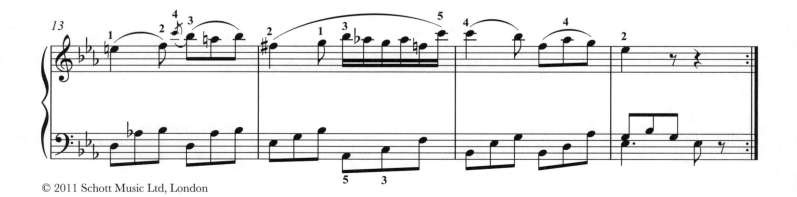

14. Scherzo

from Sonata Hob. XVI:9

Joseph Haydn
(1732–1809)

Allegro (♩ = 112)

15. Solfeggio

from Musikalische Nebenstunden

Johann Christoph F. Bach
(1732–1795)

16. Tempo di Minuetto

KV236

Wolfgang Amadeus Mozart
(1756–1791)

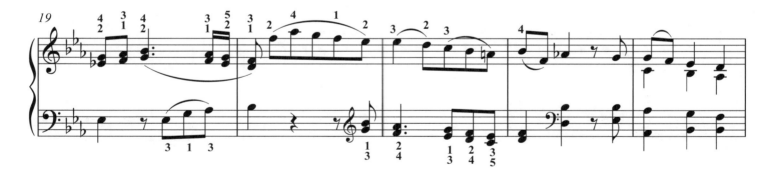

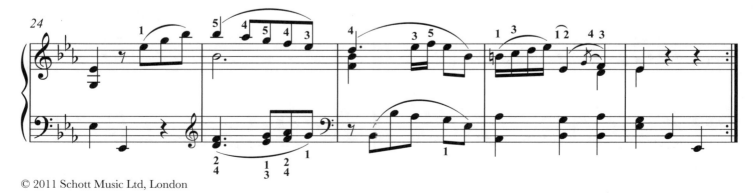

17. Arietta

from Pianoforte Method

Muzio Clementi
(1752–1832)

*) Fingering is the composer's own / Le doigté sont du compositeur / Der Fingersatz stammt von Komponisten

18. Polonaise

Op. 124 No. 3

Ferdinand Ries
(1784–1838)

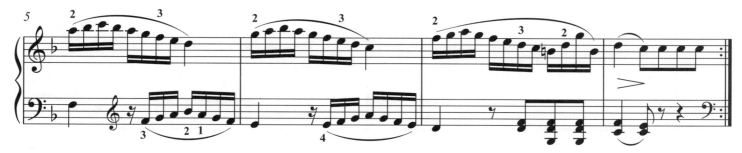

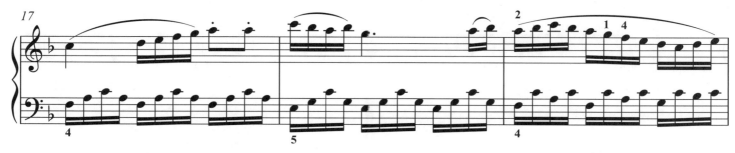

19. Andantino

Op. 453 No. 41

Carl Czerny
(1791–1857)

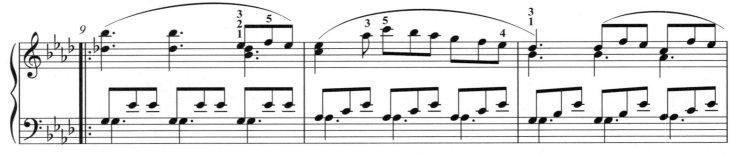

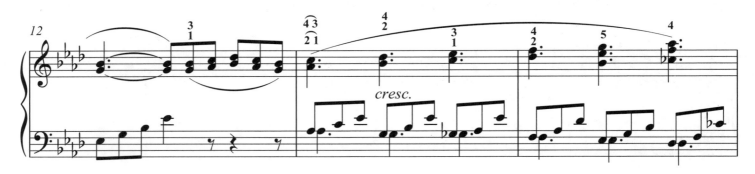

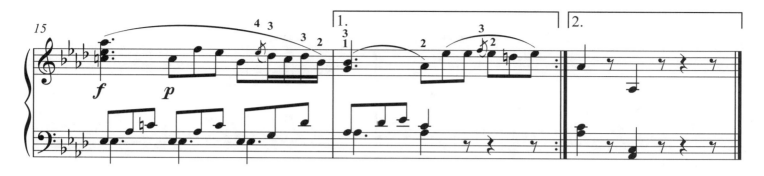

20. Romanze

Op. 52 No. 4

Johann Nepomuk Hummel
(1778-1837)

con dolcezza

[sim.]

cresc.

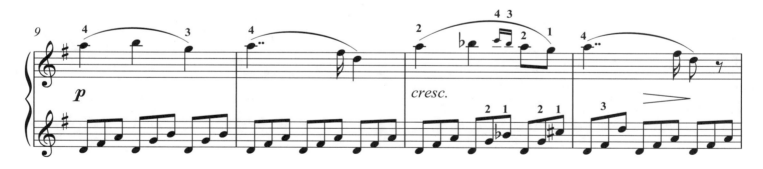

p

cresc.

21. Gigue

from Pianoforte Method

Johann Nepomuk Hummel
(1778-1837)

Allegro non troppo
(♩. = 98) *)

*) Fingering is the composer's own / Le doigté sont du compositeur / Der Fingersatz stammt von Komponisten

22. Favoritwaltzer

J. 143-8 No. 4

Carl Maria von Weber
(1786-1826)

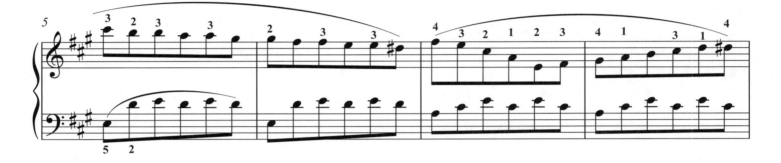

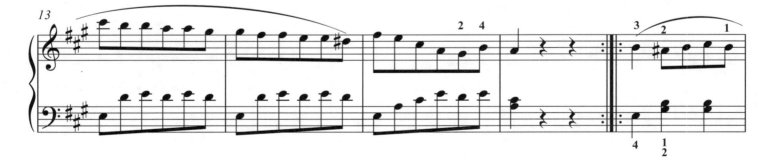

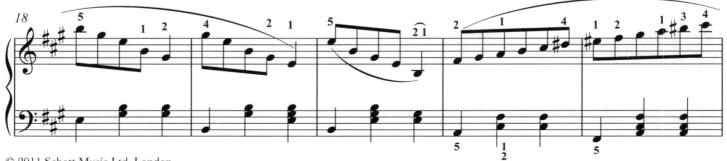

Fine

Trio
Marcato

Waltzer
D. C. al Fine

23. Favoritwaltzer

J. 143-8 No. 2

Carl Maria von Weber
(1786-1826)

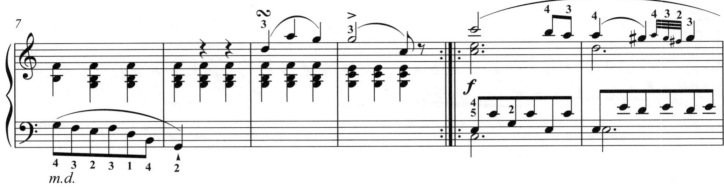

Fine

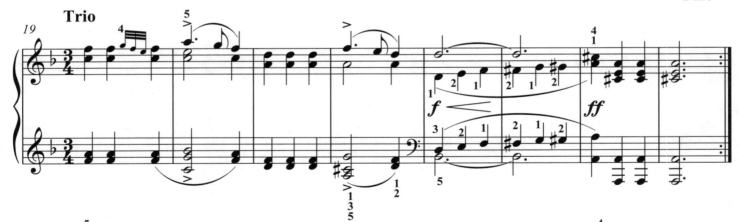

Trio

Waltzer
D. C. al Fine

24. Adagio

Hob. XVII:9

Joseph Haydn
(1732-1809)

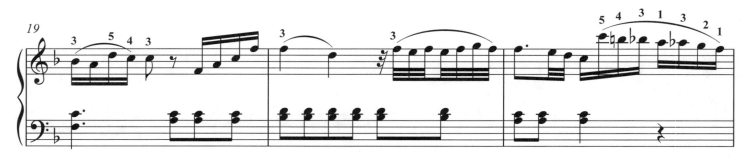

25. Klavierstück

Lustig-Traurig
WoO 54

Ludwig van Beethoven
(1770-1827)

Lustig (♩. = 60)

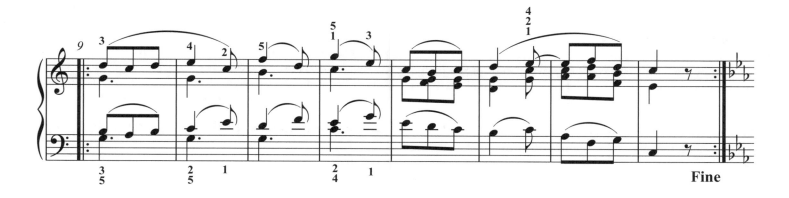

Fine

Traurig (Minore)

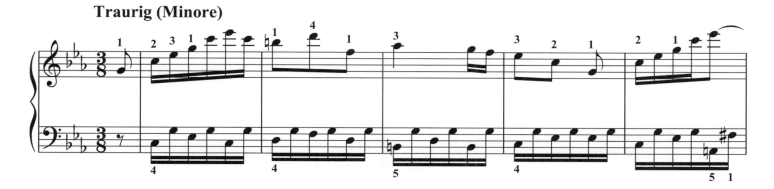

D. C. al Fine

Teaching Notes

One of the interesting challenges of playing music of this period is how we negotiate the difference between the fortepiano of the late eighteenth century and the piano of today. These differences are quite considerable, but incorporating the knowledge of period instruments while playing modern pianos can only enhance how we respond to the music. For example, the piano in the classical period had lighter keys (and fewer of them), strings that ran parallel to each other as opposed to being cross-strung, leather not felt on the hammers, slighter proportions, no metal frame (wooden instead) and a different action, too. All of this means that we can't recreate a sound as Haydn or Mozart may have heard it, but we can play the modern piano in a way that is respectful of these other musical textures. To achieve that, you might want to use sharply contrasted dynamic differences between *forte* and *piano*, and treat the right pedal as something that enhances the music at specific points, rather than being ever present. The basic sound quality should also be focused more on the treble of the instrument, rather than being bass orientated. Ornamentation too, is important and the CD recording contains the occasional ornament at a cadential point. The use of ornaments is often a matter of personal choice and so possibly the best way to think of them is as a subtle enhancing of a melody line.

Ultimately, the concept of historically informed performance practice (being aware of and influenced by an understanding of how music of a different period may have been played) is an excellent basis for experimenting with music, for listening, evaluating and decision-making.

Johann Christoph Friedrich Bach (1732–1795)

15. Solfeggio

($\quarternote = 52$)

The term *Solfeggio* means exercise, or study in this context. It's easy to see what Bach had in mind in this piece: a study in evenness, both in tempo and touch. Additionally, the piece can also be a study in composition, as each half bar (or crotchet beat in the case of bars 5–6) is based on a chord. In learning the piece, it can be useful to retrace Bach's chord progression by learning this as a sequence of harmonies before playing it as written. The inspiration for this work is likely to have been the Prelude BWV846 by Bach's father.

Ludwig van Beethoven (1770–1827)

9. Ländlerischer Tanz, WoO 11 No. 2

($\dottedquarter = 60$)

This dance is taken from a collection of seven pieces that were published in 1799. The dance character is undoubtedly enhanced by the staccato notes in the right hand. But the middle section requires a different touch, and it is the element of different forms of articulation that governs the piece. Even at the beginning, the staccato of the melody line needs to offset against a supporting non-legato touch in the left. Not easy at first, but an excellent skill to develop.

25. Klavierstück WoO54, 'Lustig-traurig'

($\dottedquarter = 60$)

The subtitle of this piano piece, *'happily and sadly'*, characterises the music and thus underlines the difference in mood between the major and minor keys. To create a sense of unity in the work, aim for one tempo that works for both sections. In the minor section, the pianistic challenge is one of togetherness between hands, while the major section needs careful voicing in the chord progressions. Also, look out for Beethoven's phrasing as it divides the music into self-contained units, not dissimilar to speech.

Domenico Cimarosa (1749–1801)

2. Sonata

($\dottedquarter = 60$)

The music makes much use of the musical repetition of two or four bar phrases but does so on the assumption of a change in dynamics, or articulation. So changes between *f* and *p* dynamics are frequent, but there are also opportunities to experiment with touch. For example, in bars 13 and 14 you could slur the first left hand quaver of each bar to the next, thus creating a dance-like 3/4 feeling. Though not notated in the score, it is perfectly within keeping of this elegant and attractive piece.

Muzio Clementi (1752–1832)

17. Arietta

($\quarternote = 92$)

This piece is piano lesson number 22 from Clementi's piano tutor book, in which he mixes his own compositions with works of other composers. It is a fascinating insight into the teaching repertoire of the eighteenth century, and it is interesting to see which skills Clementi thinks pianists ought to develop in what order. Here, it is all about coordinating quavers and semiquavers, the latter played at a lighter dynamic as a supporting texture. The cadenza in bar 16 is an important moment, and the presence of the fermata (pause) indicates that this is an improvisatory moment. At the same time, the composer's subdivision of the following notes into demisemiquavers, semiquavers, and quavers should be seen less as a restrictive notation, and more as an indication of a written-out ritardando which is given a visual framework. The ornament in bars 2 and 18 can be played as four demisemiquavers starting on B and being rhythmically aligned with their corresponding notes in the left hand.

Johann Baptist Cramer (1771–1858)

5. Guaracha

($\dottedquarter = 76$)

Cramer's comments on this piece highlight the slight emphasis he wants to have placed on the first beat of a bar, presumably to underline the dance character of this Spanish dance. These emphasised notes do help in the coordination of the semiquavers with the right hand from bar 9 onwards.

10. Praeludium & Andantino

($\quarternote = 88$) ($\dottedquarter = 52$)

Placing an introductory musical activity before a main piece, the *Andantino* in this case, was a normal part of performance practice at the time. It served several purposes: to enable the performer to focus on what was about to come, to prepare the listener for the key of the piece, and to establish or off-set the character of the subsequent material. The latter is what Cramer does here: a busy introduction may well lead to a piece in the same mood, but the beginning of the *Andantino* comes as a little bit of a surprise to an audience.

Carl Czerny (1791–1857)

13. Andante Op. 453 No. 32
(♩. = 80)
19. Andantino Op. 453 No. 41
(♩. = 76)

Both pieces by Czerny are included here because of their musical appeal, and not because of any specific technical reason. However, comparing both items shows two different approaches to creating a harmonic base on the piano. The *Andante* uses a broken chord, which, in combination with the pedal, provides the support for the melodic line. In the *Andantino*, the sustained bass note requires more careful pedalling, in order to allow a texture of three (bass, treble, inner) voices to be heard.

Carl Ditters von Dittersdorf (1739–1799)

4. English Dance No. 15
(♩ = 96)

This piece is almost like a miniature suite of dances, all combined to form one whole. The technically tricky part is the central section. In bars 9 and 11 you can use the right pedal to sustain the sound of the chord, while moving your left hand to the subsequent third. But it is the pattern of thirds in bar 15 that needs the most attention. There is a choice of fingerings in the text, and it is useful to try both, in order to find out which one works better. But if the thirds prove to be awkward in performance, here is an alternative that sounds very similar but might be more comfortable to play:

Johann Wilhelm Hässler (1747–1822)

11. Allegro assai Op. 38 No. 20
(♩ = 104)
12. Presto Op. 38 No. 29
(♩. = 86)

Both pieces are taken from a collection of short studies, each of which is concerned with a different technical challenge. No. 20 is about semiquaver passage work that is divided between both hands. No. 29 is more improvisatory in character and, though musically less self-contained than No. 20, it could easily be an early romantic piano prelude. The emphasis on the sudden changes between *f* and *p* dynamics places it firmly in a classical context. Both pieces could be useful as part of a piano warm-up or work-out routine, as they are still effective, even when played at a slightly slower tempo.

Joseph Haydn (1732–1809)

14. Scherzo Hob. XVI:9
(♩ = 112)

This *Scherzo* is the last movement of an early piano sonata, thought to have been written before 1766. Students looking for a complete sonata to learn and/or perform, can tackle the piece as a whole, though the stretch of an octave is essential for much of the left hand textures in the opening *Allegro*. (For a complete score of the other movements see Schott ED 9026.) Apart from its memorable thematic material, the attraction of the *Scherzo* is the fact that both right and left hand need to play textures that are essential

in keyboard music of this time: scales and arpeggios in the right hand, and supporting harmonic patterns in the left.

24. Adagio Hob.XVII:9
(♪ = 98)

The *Adagio* belongs to a group of *10 little piano pieces* published around 1786. All ten are transcriptions of Haydn's music, but only two, including the *Adagio*, have survived as manuscripts written out by the composer. The pulse is best felt in quavers, which does explain the overall tempo indication of the piece, as the crotchet beats will feel quite slow. In the absence of more detailed performance markings by the composer, this piece does give students and teachers quite a bit of flexibility, making it an excellent case study for experimentation with music of this period.

James Hook (1746–1827)

3. Rondo: Allegretto, from Sonatina Op. 12 No. 9
(♩ = 88)

The concept of a rondo is that it contains a central idea, which keeps returning, but is interspersed with other musical material. Hook's piece does exactly that, but in a very condensed framework. The central idea (A) appears in bars 1–8. It returns in bar 17, and as a *da capo*. The other material, are bars 9–16 (B), and bars 25–32 (C). Overall this gives an ABACA structure to the piece. As always with repetitions, you can decide whether or not you want to play something in a different way, or intentionally in the same manner. Whatever your decision, it will be the result of experimenting with articulation and dynamics. A score that is relatively blank needs the player's contribution!

Johann Nepomuk Hummel (1778–1837)

7. Allegro
(♩ = 104)

Hummel wrote this piece especially for his *Piano Method* (1828) as a musical setting for a pianistic skill that needed to be developed. It is a study in the evenness of semiquaver passage work, and just to prove that point the composer uses chords and their inversions in bars 15–16 which interrupt the pattern of the piece up to that moment. The tempo suggested allows for the bass notes to form a melodic line that gradually moves the piece towards its conclusion.

20. Romanze Op. 52 No. 4
(♩ = 84)

Hummel's *Six Pieces* Op. 52 are a collection written especially for piano students. No. 5, *Eccosaise*, which is the easiest of the set, can be found in the *Classical Piano Anthology* Vol. 1. The remaining pieces are all between Grades 4 to 5, which makes this a very useful set for students. The *Romanze* is the only lyrical work of the set. As Clementi's *Arietta* (No. 17 in this collection), Hummel's piece contains a cadential moment before the return of the main theme in bar 21.

21. Gigue
(♩. = 98)

Though predominantly associated with the music of the baroque era, the *Gigue* as a dance form still appears in the music of classical composers, such as Mozart and Hummel. The tempo of the work needs to be chosen so that the four beats per bar can be felt clearly. From a pianistic point of view, only the double notes of the last bar might be awkward. Try the following division of notes between the hands, if you find that the composer's fingering in the score does not feel (or sound) comfortable:

Wolfgang Amadeus Mozart (1756–1791)

16. Tempo di Minuetto KV236
($\bullet$ = 98)
When this work was first published in the middle of the nineteenth century, it was believed that the piece was an original composition by Mozart. However, more recent scholarhip has established that it is a piano score (by Mozart) of a melody by Christoph Willibald Gluck (1714–1787). Opinion differs on the date of Mozart's arrangement, but it is thought to date from somewhere around the early 1780s. The piece is relatively straightforward, but the basic choice of tempo is probably dependent on the time needed for the transition from bar 6 to 7.

Ferdinand Ries (1784–1838)

18. Polonaise Op. 124 No. 3
($\bullet$ = 96)
Published in 1832 as part of the *15 Easy Piano Pieces*, Ries' *Polonaise* contains textbook classical features: scale patterns in the right hand, and a rocking left hand quaver sequence at the opening that is later transformed into a semiquaver accompaniment (from bar 15 onwards). The *f* in bar 11 needs to be very firm in the articulation of both the legato semiquavers and the staccato bass notes.

Franz Schubert (1797–1828)

8. Ländler D 378 No. 3
($\bullet$. = 60)
This short *Ländler* is typical for the music of this kind. Two halves of eight bars each, based on an often predictable sequence of harmonies. Schubert's skill, if not genius, was to take these patterns and to create works of seemingly unlimited melodic variety. In the case of this dance, the right hand needs to be articulated in groups of two quavers, whether they are *staccato* or *legato*. In the repeat of the second half, you could give less weight to the dotted minims the first time round, but emphasise them in the repeat.

Georg Christoph Wagenseil (1715–1777)

1. Allegro, from Divertimento No. 2
($\bullet$. = 66–72)
This *Allegro* is an effective piece for the learning of terraced dynamics. The performance indications in the score are entirely editorial, and as such discretionary, but they enable you to highlight what, at the time, was new about the pianoforte as opposed to the harpsichord: the ability to play loudly and softly through an adjustment of touch. It is very likely that at the time of composition this music was still being played on the harpsichord, but only some 15–20 years later musical tastes (and instrument making) were changing.
This piece by Wagenseil could be a useful preliminary study to Haydn's *Scherzo* in the same key (No. 14 in this collection).

Carl Maria von Weber (1786–1826)

Weber's most successful piano piece, *Invitation to the Dance* Op. 65, was one of the most popular and enduring piano items in the nineteenth century. Subject to numerous 'concert arrangements' by various piano virtuosi, it linked the composer's name with the dance form as a genre. Somewhat surprisingly, Weber's small dance pieces never attracted the same attention, though many of them are rather effective pieces in their own right. The two waltzes in this anthology both date from 1812, and are part of a set of six that were written at the request of the music publisher A. Kühnel.

22. Favoritwaltzer J. 143–8 No. 4
($\bullet$. = 63)
The repeated notes in bars 5–6 are a typical feature of Weber's piano writing. He used this not only in his smaller works, but also in concert repertoire such as the piano sonata Op. 24. Listen to the quavers in both hands very carefully, as they need to be assembled very precisely. The arpeggiated bass notes in the *Trio* must be a nod to Mozart's *Rondo alla turca* in the latter's piano sonata KV 331!

23. Favoritwaltzer J. 143–8 No. 2
($\bullet$. = 58)
This may be a rather personal perspective, but if charm and drama could be combined on one page, this must surely be it. Both *Waltz* and *Trio* are based on a light-hearted first half, and a more dramatic second. The ornament in bar 12 can be played as a group of four semiquavers on the last beat of the bar.

Samuel Wesley (1766– 1837)

6. Vivace, from Sonatina Op. 12 No. 8
($\bullet$ = 88)
Only the slur in bar 4 is given in the work's edition of c. 1799; all other performance indications are editorial. For the purpose of this recording, I have decided to play the semiquavers in this piece in two different ways in order to create a variety of touch: bars 1–8 and 17–24 are *staccato*, and bars 9–16 are played as *non-legato* notes. But this is a suggestion only. The score has deliberately been left blank, so that you can write in your own performance directions for this work. In bars 9–14 all semiquaver patterns followed by a quaver cover a five note sequence, hence the fingering I have suggested. Again, if a suggested pattern does not feel comfortable for your hand, change it.

Biographical Notes

Johann Christoph Friedrich Bach (1732–1795)

Johann Christoph Friedrich Bach was taught by his father Johann Sebastian while attending the *Thomasschule* in Leipzig. He was subsequently appointed as the court harpsichordist in Bückeburg, a region that was to play an important part throughout his life. By 1759 J. C. Bach was the *Kapellmeister* of the local court orchestra. In 1778 he applied for permission to visit his brother Johann Christian Bach in London, where he published six keyboard concertos and a set of string quartets. He returned from London with an English fortepiano, and it is therefore possible, if not likely, that keyboard music written after that point was intended for this instrument, rather than the harpsichord. Bach was also in demand as a teacher, and his students included the future Mozart-scholar and *Thomaskantor* August Eberhard Müller (see Schott *Classical Piano Anthology* Vol. 1).

Ludwig van Beethoven (1770–1827)

Beethoven's influence on the direction of music in his time, as well as on the musical developments of subsequent composers, was considerable and multi-layered. His own stylistic development as a composer has resulted in the categorising of his output into three distinct periods: up to about 1802 (early), from 1802–1812 (middle), and from 1812 onwards (late). In terms of Beethoven's piano writing, these periods reflect the classical heritage of his initial phase, the development of his virtuoso keyboard style, and the subsequent structural, as well as technical individuality of his later works.

As a composer, Beethoven excelled in almost all forms of instrumental music, from the string quartet, the piano sonata, to the concerto and the symphony. The spontaneity, strength and emotional impact of his music were nevertheless the result of a meticulously crafted process of composition that is documented in detail in his sketchbooks and autographs. Beethoven was a successful performer as a pianist, though contemporary accounts of his playing differ in their assessment, depending on the focus of the writers. While some praised Beethoven's power and sound projection, others thought his playing to be messy and lacking control. What most sources agree upon though, is the impact Beethoven's playing made upon his listeners.

A piano work that unites both perspectives of his playing is the *Fantasy* for piano Op. 77; a work that is largely understood to be the written down version of an improvisation. It contains many Beethovenian features in harmony, melody and texture, and can as such offer a unique insight into the workings of this great musician.

Beethoven's compositional achievements were so considerable that subsequent generations of composers from Schubert to Schumann, Liszt and Brahms hesitated for some time before writing in a genre that Beethoven had previously made his own.

Domenico Cimarosa (1749–1801)

Cimarosa is best remembered as a highly successful composer of operas. After training as a singer, violinist and keyboard player in his native Naples, the growing popularity of his operas enabled him to move from Naples to Venice, then to the Russian court at St. Petersburg where he worked from 1787–1791, and on to Vienna before returning to Naples in 1793. His pro-republican views caused problems for Cimarosa in the politically volatile Italy of the 1790s, and after brief imprisonment in 1799 he returned to Venice where he died in 1801.

Cimarosa's stage works were held in high regard by many of his contemporaries. Haydn is known to have conducted several of Cimarosa's operas, but the reception of his keyboard works is less well documented. Most of the keyboard sonatas are one-movement works, and many use binary form. Their transparent style, combined with the structural format, does invite comparisons with Scarlatti's keyboard sonatas, though the melodic material places them firmly in the classical period.

Muzio Clementi (1752–1832)

Clementi was born in Rome but moved to England in 1766 at the instigation of Peter Beckford (1740–92) on whose estate in Dorset Clementi spent the next seven years. In 1774 Clementi moved to London before starting a continental concert tour in 1780. In 1782 Mozart wrote to his father about Clementi's playing which he criticised for being too mechanical, despite admiring his playing of thirds. By 1785 Clementi was back in London where he remained until 1802, having diversified his commercial activities from teacher/performer to include also those of publisher, conductor and piano maker. Clementi's life continued to be a mixture of diverse musical activities (including foreign tours) though gradually his business responsibilities took over more of his time. He retired in 1830.

Clementi taught a number of successful pianst-composers, including Johann Baptist Cramer, John Field and Frederic Kalkbrenner. His understanding of, and contribution to, the development of pianism is evident in two principal publications, the Introduction to the *Art of Playing on the Piano Forte* (a tutor book) and the *Gradus at Parnassum*, a collection of pieces designed to promote more advanced pianism.

Johann Baptist Cramer (1771–1858)

Born in Germany, Cramer was taken to England at the age of three by his family. In 1783 he studied with Muzio Clementi for a year, whose style of piano playing became a major influence on Cramer in the development of his own pianism. Indeed, Cramer became known amongst colleagues and audiences for the quality of his legato touch. As Clementi did before him, Cramer managed to combine a career as a performer, teacher and musical businessman, becoming involved in music publishing from 1805 onwards. These seemingly diverse roles were not uncommon amongst musicians in the second half of the eighteenth century, especially as the writing and publishing of educational music in particular was a lucrative market. Cramer's *84 Studies* for piano (published in two sets of 42 in 1804 and 1810), aimed at just such an audience, were as commercially successful as they were pianistically influential. Beethoven recommended them for the development of piano technique (he annotated selected Cramer Etudes, highlighting their individual musical purposes), Schumann used them, Henselt composed a second piano part to them, and Liszt's student Carl Tausig (one of the nineteenth century's most celebrated pianists) edited a selection of Cramer Etudes, thus underlining their relevance about half a century after they first appeared in print.

Cramer's life pre 1800 seems to have consisted of teaching piano and going on concert tours across parts of Europe. Post 1800, he remained mostly England-based, concentrating on his music publishing business and composition. Cramer retired in 1835 as a highly respected member of London's musical life.

Carl Czerny (1791–1857)

Czerny was, and remains, a significant figure in the development of pianism. Though predominantly remembered for being Beethoven's student and Liszt's teacher, Carl Czerny was an interesting composer in his own right. The systematic approach in which he developed his own collections of piano exercises was identical with the meticulous way in which he documented his studies with Beethoven, and his early impressions of Liszt. Unsurprisingly, it is in this context that he is mostly remembered.

Czerny's own skills as a composer are possibly best encapsulated in two of his earlier works, the piano sonata Op. 7 (performed by Liszt in Paris in 1830) and his highly dramatic symphony in C minor. Aged 16, Czerny decided not to pursue a career as a performer, but to devote himself to teaching instead. This he did, often working for ten hours or more per day until he retired from teaching in 1836.

Czerny left arguably the most comprehensive teaching legacy of any pianist-tutor of his era, as set out in his *Pianoforte-Schule* Op. 500, a work he updated in 1846.

Carl Ditters von Dittersdorf (1739–1799)

Dittersdorf was an Austrian violinist and composer who nowadays is mostly remembered for music other than for keyboard. His extensive output includes oratorios, symphonies, chamber music, encapsulating almost every genre he came into contact with. This was almost certainly due to his professional duties as a *Kapellmeister* and impresario. Dittersdorf performed as a violinist with Gluck on tour in Italy in 1763 before accepting an appointment as *Kapellmeister* to the Bishop of Grosswardein, where he succeeded Michael Haydn (the brother of Joseph Haydn). After a period of political uncertainty in the 1770s, Dittersdorf enjoyed renewed success in Vienna in the second half of the 1780s, a period in which he also travelled to Berlin for performances of his works.

Dittersdorf's music enjoyed considerable popularity, so much so that it is still difficult to verify his authorship of some works.

Johann Wilhelm Hässler (1747–1822)

Born in Erfurt in 1747, Hässler became a student of his uncle, the Erfurt organist Johann Christian Kittel. By the age of 16, Hässler held his first appointment as an organist in Erfurt but soon began to travel across Germany as a concertizing musician. In 1780 he founded his own music publishing business and by 1790 had travelled as far afield as England and Russia, where he became the court conductor in St. Petersburg in 1792. In a letter from 1788, the poet and writer Friedrich von Schiller recalls Hässler's playing: 'He plays like a master and composes very well. As a person, he is an original and a rather fiery being.' [1] From 1794 onwards, Hässler lived in Moscow where he worked as a highly respected and sought-after piano teacher. His contribution to the development of Russian pianism in the first half of the nineteenth century is yet to be defined but most of his published works for piano suggest a clear focus on developing the skills of less experienced players. Hässler's own keyboard style developed from the piano writing of C. P. E. Bach but shares the accessibility of Haydn's earlier piano sonatas. Many of Hässler's smaller teaching pieces and easier piano sonatas benefit from their immediate musical appeal, and his piano method contains many works that can still be used today.

Joseph Haydn (1732–1809)

The evaluation of Haydn's position as a composer has undergone a number of changes over time. A popular perception of Haydn's life is the focus on the relative comfort and stability of his almost 30 year employment by the Esterhazy family in Eisenstadt near Vienna. Despite this comparatively settled existence (at least compared to that of many of his contemporaries, not least Mozart), Haydn's music was published widely post 1780, gaining its composer a growing national and international reputation. Visits to London from 1791 onwards confirmed his musical and economic successes.

However, his early years were very different. After initial training as a chorister and violinist, Haydn, who was not a virtuoso performer, survived by teaching and playing in ad hoc ensembles that provided music for functions. Compositionally, Haydn progressed slowly from being essentially self-taught to gaining the necessary skills. From the mid 1760s onwards Haydn developed a more distinctive musical style.

Haydn's output for piano covers over 60 sonatas, individual pieces, and variations. Though not a virtuoso keyboard performer, Haydn knew exactly how to write effectively for the fortepiano. All of his works lie very well under the fingers (irrespective of their varying degrees of complexity), but it is the element of surprise, both harmonically and in terms of pianistic textures, that gives many of the pieces their particular charm. Haydn's piano writing is never formulaic and therefore ever so slightly unpredictable.

James Hook (1746–1827)

Hook's musical talent seemed to have been evident very early in his life. By the age of six he performed concerti in public, and aged eight is reported to have written his first large-scale works though these are considered lost today.

After moving to London in 1764, Hook held a succession of posts as organist in the London area, composing vocal music, including operas, and teaching privately as a sought-after keyboard tutor. His activities as a teacher explain much of his educational keyboard music which is both elegant and technically rewarding. The *Sonatinas* Op. 12 were published in 1775.

Johann Nepomuk Hummel (1778–1837)

Hummel was arguably a pivotal figure in his time, both pianistically and compositionally. A pupil of Mozart, Hummel's music always retained its classical roots in terms of its structure and musical detail. Yet as a pianist, and maybe most importantly as an influential piano teacher, Hummel trained many exponents of the first generation of nineteenth century pianism: Henselt, Hiller, Mendelssohn and Thalberg all benefitted from Hummel's tuition. Other pianists of the time were also influenced by Hummel. Schumann considered studying with him (he didn't in the end) but Hummel's decorative right hand figurations clearly occupied Schumann, as the Abegg *Variations* Op. 1 and other early works document. Liszt, too, came into contact with Hummel's music by playing the latter's Piano Concerti Opp. 85 and 89 early on in his career as a travelling virtuoso. Even Chopin must have been familiar with Hummel's works, as some of his earlier works display some stylistic, occasionally even melodic, similarities.

One of Hummel's outstanding achievements is his piano method of 1828, a 450+ page document that claims to train the student 'from the first lesson to the most complete training' [2]. Published by Tobias Haslinger in Vienna, it is possibly the nineteenth century's first comprehensive piano method book that established the technical concepts upon which the virtuoso pianism of that century was based. Hummel's thorough training methodology apart, what makes this method quite remarkable is its author's awareness of and perspective on aspects of pedagogy: student-teacher interaction, motivation, and lesson delivery are amongst the topics that Hummel explores.

Wolfgang Amadeus Mozart (1756–1791)

Mozart was born into a highly musical environment. His father Leopold worked as an orchestral violinist and educator in Salzburg, and his older sister Nannerl had already shown her ability as a keyboard player. Mozart made rapid progress in his musical studies, so much so that his father decided to take him on a concert tour through Germany to London and Paris. These travels lasted for three and a half years before Mozart settled into life in Salzburg in 1766. Annual travels to Italy followed from 1769–72, enabling Mozart to come into contact with many other musicians, as indeed he did throughout his life. By the early 1780s Mozart seemed to have settled into life as a freelance musician in all its diversity. Some of his most successful piano concerti date from this period, as do many string quartets, some of which he played alongside their dedicatee, Joseph Haydn. By the end of the decade (and the beginning of the next) Mozart enjoyed considerable success as an opera composer with works such as *Cosi fan tutte* and *Die Zauberflöte*.

The diversity of Mozart's keyboard writing naturally reflects the different periods in the composer's life. Some of the earliest works date from when he was only five, a time when he wrote mostly shorter dances. His mature works include sonatas, variations and individual pieces, many of them written for his own use.

Ferdinand Ries (1784–1838)

Ries received his earliest musical training as a pianist and violinist from his father, Franz Ries. In 1801 Ferdinand worked as a music copyist in Munich in an attempt to finance further study before moving on to Vienna a year later. In Vienna he studied piano with Beethoven for three years, and composition with Albrechtsberger. Beethoven was a significant help to Ries in the commencing of his career as a travelling virtuoso, and for the subsequent decade Ries appeared as a performer all over Europe. By 1813 he arrived in London, only to stay in England for 14 years. In 1814 he married an English woman. Ries' period in England seemed to have been the most stable, and financially secure of his life. Retiring in 1824,

1) Kahl, W., *Selbstbiographien Deutscher Musiker* (Koeln und Krefeld, Staufen Verlag, 1948), p. 47
2) Hummel, J. N., *Anweisung zum Piano-forte spielen* (Wien: Haslinger, 1828)

he moved back to Germany, initially Godesberg and some three years later, Frankfurt.

Ries' music essentially retained its classical roots throughout his creative output. His most successful work for piano was his piano concerto in C sharp minor Op. 55.

Franz Schubert (1797–1828)

Schubert's initial musical training was provided by his father and brothers who taught him to play the piano, violin and viola. Aged 11 he was awarded a choral scholarship that enabled him to study with Salieri. By the age of 16, Schubert decided to train as a teacher and a year later started work at his father's school. Aged 17, Schubert had written some of his early masterpieces, *Erlkönig* and *Gretchen am Spinnrade* for voice and piano. In 1816 Schubert relinquished his teaching post, choosing instead to live in the Viennese city centre and concentrating on composition. A period of financial uncertainty followed, but late in 1819 Schubert wrote his first larger scale chamber music masterpiece, the *Trout quintet*. In spring 1821 the success of the *Erlkönig* led to publications of his songs by Diabelli, and from it Schubert experienced a brief period of financial stability. From 1820–23 he was preoccupied by writing operatic music, a less than successful venture, only to turn to writing chamber and symphonic works for the last three years of his life.

Schubert's piano writing is, with few exceptions, not preoccupied with some of the outwardly technical components that some of his contemporaries employed. Instead, much of the music's demands arise from its preference of musical purpose over any form of pianistic consideration.

Georg Christoph Wagenseil (1715–1777)

Wagenseil's historical importance stems from his activities as a composer and teacher at the Austrian court. In his capacity as an all-round musician, he influenced a younger generation of composers such as J. A. Steffan (see Schott *Classical Piano Anthology* Vol. 3) and F. X. Dusek and was therefore highly influential in the formation of the emerging Classical style post 1750. His four sets of keyboard divertimenti Op.1–4 were published between 1753 and 1763 and enjoyed an immediate success. The six year old Mozart played one of Wagenseil's concerti in public in 1762, indicative of the composer's standing in his time. Unsurprisingly, there are some textural similarities between the keyboard writing of Wagenseil and Mozart's early note books. And yet Wagenseil's style was more than a mere stepping-stone to the classical era. The elegance of his music was based on writing effectively for learners, as is documented in his position as *Hofklaviermeister* from 1749 onwards.

Carl Maria von Weber (1786–1826)

Weber's early life is typical of that of many musicians of his time. Receiving his initial musical instruction from his father and several local musicians, Weber's travels around Germany and Austria put him in touch with Michael Haydn (Joseph's brother and a highly respected composer in his own right) and the composer and theorist Georg Joseph Vogler who provided much of the systematic tuition Weber needed. Until 1810, Weber moved from place to place, holding down a succession of musical and, in some cases, administrative positions. A court case against him and his father, being placed under civil arrest and, ultimately, banned from the area of Würtenberg had a profound effect on Weber. Determined to change his life, he embarked on two years of composing, concertizing and living within his means. Appointments as court and/or theatre conductor soon followed; Prague from 1813–16 and Dresden from 1817–1821; periods during which he also continued to travel as a performing musician. Arguably the most significant change in Weber's life occurred due to the extraordinary popularity of his opera *Der Freischütz* (1820), a work that secured him success throughout Germany, as well as internationally.

Weber's piano writing is distinctive, yet also difficult to summarise. It is clearly melodically driven, as is much of Weber's homophonic writing, with a particular emphasis on dance forms and dotted rhythmic patterns that underpin his compositional style. As a pianist, Weber is drawn to elaborate and often virtuosic right hand writing; fast moving chord progressions, hand crossing and leaps that go far beyond a hand position. In that sense, Weber's piano writing is based on the fluid scale and arpeggio technique favoured by Hummel, but occupies a half way position between the latter and the pianism demanded by Chopin and Liszt from the 1830s onwards.

Samuel Wesley (1766–1837)

Samuel Wesley was a brilliant but partly controversial figure in the musical life of his time. Born in Bristol, his parents moved to London in 1771 where the family home in Marylebone proved to be an excellent platform for Wesley's early display of his musical skills. William Boyce's remark in 1774, labelling the young musician as an 'English Mozart' is indicative of these early successes. Principally an organist, Wesley's musical activities were typical of musicians of his time. He earned a living through a mixture of private teaching, performance and composition work. Though immensely respected in his musical activities, Wesley's non-conformist personal life and his frequent periods of depression prevented him from ever being at the centre of English musical life. Unfortunately, a sizeable part of Wesley's keyboard music remains unavailable today, despite its accessible style and freshness of invention.

Nils Franke

Bibliography

Hinson, Maurice.
Guide to the Pianist's Repertoire.
Bloomington and Indianapolis: Indiana University Press, 2000

MacGrath, Jane.
The Pianist's Guide to Standard Teaching and Performance Literature.
Van Nuys: Alfred Publishing Co., 1995

Prosnitz, Adolf.
Handbuch der Klavierliteratur.
Wien: Doblinger, 1908

Sadie, Stanley (ed.)
Grove Concise Dictionary of Music.
London: MacMillan Publishers, 1988

Sadie, Stanley (ed.)
Grove Dictionary of Music online.
[accessed 04/04/2011]

Wolters, Klaus.
Handbuch der Klavierliteratur zu zwei Händen.
Zürich and Mainz: Atlantis Musikbuch Verlag, 2001

Notes pédagogiques

L'un des enjeux intéressants dans l'interprétation de la musique de cette période réside dans la négociation des différences entre le pianoforte de la fin du 18e siècle et le piano actuel. Ces différences sont assez considérables, mais l'intégration de notre connaissance des instruments d'époque ne peut qu'enrichir la réponse que nous apportons à cette musique lorsque nous la jouons sur un piano moderne. Par exemple, les touches du piano de la période classique étaient plus légères (et moins nombreuses), ses cordes disposées parallèlement et non croisées, ses marteaux recouverts de cuir et non de feutre ; il était de proportions plus réduites, n'avait pas de cadre métallique et possédait également un autre mécanisme. Cela signifie que nous ne pouvons recréer les sonorités telles que Mozart ou Haydn les entendaient, mais nous pouvons jouer du piano moderne en respectant ces textures musicales différentes. Afin d'y parvenir, il vous faudra user de contrastes dynamiques très différenciés entre *piano* et *forte* et traiter la pédale de droite comme un moyen d'enrichir ponctuellement la musique plutôt que de l'utiliser en permanence. Fondamentalement, la qualité sonore devra être axée davantage sur les aigus de l'instrument que sur les graves. L'ornementation est également importante et l'enregistrement figurant sur le CD contient des ornementations occasionnelles dans les passages cadentiels. L'utilisation des ornements est souvent une question de choix personnel dans l'enrichissement subtil d'une ligne mélodique.

Enfin, le concept d'une pratique musicale historiquement éclairée (conscience et influence de la compréhension des pratiques musicales d'une époque différente) constitue une base excellente à l'expérimentation musicale, pour l'écoute, l'évaluation et les choix musicaux.

Johann Christoph Friedrich Bach (1732–1795)
15. Solfeggio
($\downarrow$ = 52)

Dans ce contexte, le terme de *Solfeggio* signifie exercice ou étude. Il est aisé de comprendre ce que Bach avait en tête avec ce morceau : une étude sur la régularité, à la fois dans le tempo et le toucher. Cette pièce peut également servir à l'étude des procédés d'écriture, chaque demi-mesure (ou noire dans le cas des mesures 5–6) reposant sur un accord différent. Quand vous travaillerez cette pièce, avant de la jouer telle qu'elle est écrite, il pourra être utile de retracer la progression des accords de Bach, prenant ainsi conscience qu'il s'agit d'une séquence harmonique. Il est probable le *Prélude* BWV 846 de son père ait été la source d'inspiration du compositeur.

Ludwig van Beethoven (1770–1827)
9. Ländlerischer Tanz, WoO 11 no 2
($\downarrow$ = 60)

Cette danse est tirée d'un recueil de sept pièces qui furent publiées en 1799. Son caractère dansant est indubitablement rehaussé par les notes *staccato* de la main droite. Mais la partie centrale requiert un toucher différent, et ce sont ces différentes formes d'articulation qui gouvernent la pièce. Même au début, le *staccato* de la ligne mélodique doit trouver un équilibre avec le toucher détaché de l'accompagnement de la main droite. Ce n'est pas facile au premier abord, mais constitue une excellente compétence à développer.

25. Klavierstück WoO54, 'Lustig-traurig'
($\downarrow$. = 60)

Le sous-titre de cette pièce, « gaiment et tristement », caractérise la musique et souligne ainsi la différence d'atmosphère entre tonalité majeure et mineure. Afin de donner à l'œuvre une certaine unité, recherchez un tempo adapté aux deux parties. Dans la partie en mode mineur, l'homogénéité entre les mains constitue le principal enjeu pianistique, tandis que la partie en mode majeur nécessite d'accorder un soin particulier à la réalisation des voix à l'intérieur de la progression des accords. Prêtez également attention au phrasé de Beethoven dans la mesure où il subdivise la musique en unités autonomes, d'une manière rappelant le langage parlé.

Domenico Cimarosa (1749–1801)
2. Sonata
($\downarrow$ = 60)

Cette œuvre fait un large usage de la répétition de phrases musicales de deux ou quatre mesures, tout en misant manifestement sur des changements de dynamique ou d'articulation. Ainsi, les passages de **f** à **p** sont fréquents, mais d'autres occasions de varier le toucher existent aussi. Par exemple, aux mesures 13 et 14 à la main gauche, vous pouvez effectuer une liaison de phrasé entre la première croche de chaque mesure et la suivante, créant ainsi la sensation d'un 3/4, comme s'il s'agissait d'une danse. Bien qu'il ne soit pas noté dans la partition, cet effet est tout à fait en accord avec l'esprit de cette pièce attractive et élégante.

Muzio Clementi (1752–1832)
17. Arietta
($\downarrow$ = 92)

Cette pièce est la leçon de piano numéro 22 de la méthode de piano de Clementi, dans laquelle il mêle ses propres compositions à celles d'autres compositeurs. Cette méthode offre un aperçu fascinant sur le répertoire pédagogique du piano au dix-huitième siècle et il est intéressant de voir quelles sont les qualités dont Clementi pensait qu'elles devaient être développées par les pianistes, et dans quel ordre. Ici, il s'agit de coordonner croches et doubles-croches, ces dernières devant être exécutées de manière plus légère du fait de leur rôle d'accompagnement. La cadence de la mesure 16 constitue un moment important et la présence du point d'orgue indique qu'il s'agit d'un passage réservé à l'improvisation.

Parallèlement, le procédé utilisé par le compositeur de subdivision des notes qui suivent le point d'orgue en triples croches, doubles croches puis croches devra être considéré moins comme une notation restrictive que comme l'indication développée dans l'écriture d'un ritardando auquel est conféré un cadre visuel. Les ornements des mesures 2 et 18 peuvent être joués comme quatre doubles croches en commençant sur si et alignées rythmiquement sur les notes correspondantes à la main gauche.

Johann Baptist Cramer (1771–1858)
5. Guaracha
($\downarrow$ = 76)

Les commentaires de Cramer sur cette pièce révèlent la légère emphase qu'il souhaite voir appliquée sur le premier temps de chaque mesure, sans doute pour souligner le caractère dansant de cette danse espagnole. Ces notes accentuées facilitent la coordination des doubles croches de la main gauche avec la main droite à partir de la mesure 9.

10. Prélude & Andantino
(♩ = 88) (♩. = 52)

Dans la pratique instrumentale de cette époque, il était normal de faire précéder la pièce principale, ici l'*Andantino*, d'une petite activité musicale d'introduction. Cette dernière avait plusieurs objectifs : permettre à l'interprète de se concentrer sur ce qui l'attendait ensuite, préparer l'auditeur à la tonalité de la pièce et esquisser ou installer le caractère du matériau à suivre. C'est ce dernier effet qu'utilise Cramer dans le cas présent : une introduction animée est censée conduire à une pièce de même caractère. Cependant, dans ce cas précis, le début de l'*Andantino* réserve une petite surprise à l'auditoire.

Carl Czerny (1791–1857)

13. Andante op. 453 no 32
(♩. = 80)
19. Andantino op. 453 no 41
(♩. = 76)

La présence de ces deux pièces de Czerny dans le présent recueil tient davantage à leur attrait musical qu'à une quelconque raison technique. Cependant, leur comparaison dévoile deux approches différentes dans la création d'une base harmonique au piano. L'*Andante* utilise l'accord brisé, qui, allié à la pédale, procure le soutien de la ligne mélodique. Dans l'*Andantino*, la note de basse soutenue requiert un jeu de pédale plus attentif afin de permettre d'entendre la texture à trois voix (basse, soprano et voix intermédiaire).

Karl Ditters von Dittersdorf (1739–1799)

4. Danse anglaise no 15
(♩ = 96)

Cette pièce se présente quasiment comme une suite de danses miniature, combinées pour former un ensemble. La partie centrale comporte quelques difficultés techniques. Aux mesures 9 et 11, vous pouvez utiliser la pédale de droite afin de soutenir le son de l'accord tout en déplaçant votre main gauche vers la tierce suivante. Mais c'est le motif de tierces de la mesure 15 qui requiert le plus d'attention. Deux doigtés différents vous sont proposés dans la partition, et il est utile de les tester afin de trouver lequel fonctionne le mieux. Si les tierces restent malgré tout difficiles à exécuter, voici une alternative qui sonne de manière très similaire, mais sera peut-être plus confortable :

Johann Wilhelm Hässler (1747–1822)

11. Allegro assai op. 38 no 20
(♩ = 104)
12. Presto op. 38 no29
(♩. = 86)

Ces deux pièces sont tirées d'un recueil de courtes études abordant chacune une difficulté technique différente. Le no 20 s'attache aux passages en doubles croches partagés entre les deux mains. Le caractère du no 29 tient davantage de l'improvisation. Bien que moins abouti musicalement que le no 20, il pourrait très bien s'agir d'un

prélude des débuts du romantisme. Cependant, l'accent mis sur les passages soudains de **p** à **f** le place clairement dans un contexte classique. Restant efficaces même à un tempo plus lent que celui indiqué, ces deux pièces peuvent également trouver une utilité en tant qu'échauffements ou comme exercices de routine.

Joseph Haydn (1732–1809)

14. Scherzo Hob. XVI:9
(♩ = 112)

Ce scherzo constitue le dernier mouvement d'une des premières sonates pour piano de Haydn dont on pense qu'il l'a écrite avant 1766. Les élèves désireux d'apprendre et/ou de jouer une sonate complète peuvent aborder la pièce dans son ensemble, bien que l'écart d'une octave soit un élément essentiel de la plupart des textures de la main gauche dans l'*Allegro* d'ouverture (Schott ED 9026 pour la partition complète des autres mouvements). Hormis son matériau thématique particulier, l'attrait de ce scherzo réside en ce que les textures musicales des deux mains constituent des éléments essentiels de la musique pour piano de cette époque : gammes et arpèges à la main droite, motifs harmoniques en soutien à la main gauche.

24. Adagio Hob.XVII:9
(♪ = 98)

L'*Adagio* appartient à un groupe *10 petites pièces pour piano* publiées autour de 1786. Ces dix pièces sont toutes des transcriptions d'œuvres de Haydn, mais seules deux d'entre elles nous sont parvenues sous la forme de manuscrits de la main du compositeur. La pulsation aura avantage à être ressentie à la croche, ce qui explique l'indication générale de tempo, les temps à la noire paraissant plutôt lents. En l'absence d'indications plus détaillées du compositeur, cette pièce laisse aux élèves et professeurs une certaine flexibilité, fournissant ainsi une excellente opportunité d'expérimenter la musique de cette période.

James Hook (1746–1827)

3. Rondo : Allegretto, de la sonatine op. 12 no 9
(♩ = 88)

Le concept du rondo est qu'il contient une idée principale revenant plusieurs fois, à laquelle sont intercalés d'autres matériaux musicaux. C'est exactement le cas de cette pièce de Hook, mais dans un cadre très condensé. L'idée principale (A) occupe les mesures 1 à 8. Elle revient mesure 17 puis sous forme de Da capo. L'autre matériau figure mesures 9 à 16 (B) et mesures 25 à 32 (C). Globalement, cela donne à la pièce une structure ABACA. Comme toujours lorsqu'il y a des répétitions, vous pouvez choisir de varier ou non. Quelle que soit votre décision, elle sera le résultat des expérimentations auxquelles vous aurez procédé en termes d'articulation et de dynamique. Une partition relativement peu chargée requiert la contribution de l'interprète !

Johann Nepomuk Hummel (1778–1837)

7. Allegro
(♩ = 104)

Hummel écrivit cette pièce spécialement pour sa méthode de piano (1828) donnant ainsi un cadre musical à une compétence pianistique qu'il souhaitait voir développer. Il s'agit d'une étude sur la régularité des passages en doubles croches, et pour le démontrer, le compositeur introduit aux mesures 15–16 des accords et leurs renversements interrompant le motif présent jusqu'à ce moment-là. Le tempo suggéré permet aux notes de la basse de former une ligne mélodique conduisant progressivement la pièce jusqu'à à sa conclusion.

20. Romanze op. 52 no 4
($\downarrow$ = 84)

Les Six pièces op. 52 de Hummel sont un recueil écrit spécifiquement dans un but pédagogique. Le no5, *Écossaise*, qui est la pièce la plus facile de l'ensemble, figure dans le volume 1 de l'*Anthologie du piano classique*. Les autres pièces se situent toutes entre les niveaux 4 et 5, ce qui en fait une série très utile pour les élèves pianistes. Comme l'Arietta de Clementi (no17 du présent recueil), la pièce de Hummel contient un passage cadentiel avant le retour du thème principal de la mesure 21.

21. Gigue
($\downarrow$. = 98)

Bien qu'associée principalement à la musique de la période baroque, la gigue en tant que danse continue à figurer dans la musique de compositeurs classiques tels que Mozart et Hummel. Le tempo de l'œuvre sera choisi de telle sorte que les quatre pulsations à la mesure puissent être clairement ressenties. D'un point de vue pianistique, seules les doubles notes de la dernière mesure peuvent sembler difficiles. Si vous trouvez les doigtés du compositeur dans la partition trop inconfortables, ou si cela ne sonne pas comme vous le souhaitez, testez la répartition des notes entre les deux mains telle qu'elle est proposée ci-dessous :

Wolfgang Amadeus Mozart (1756–1791)
16. Tempo di Minuetto KV236
($\downarrow$ = 98)

Lorsque cette œuvre fut publiée pour la première fois au milieu du dix-neuvième siècle, on pensait qu'il s'agissait d'une composition originale de Mozart. Cependant, des recherches plus récentes ont établi qu'il s'agit d'une partition pour piano (de Mozart) sur une mélodie de Christoph Willibald Gluck (1714–1787). Les avis divergent quant à la date de l'arrangement de Mozart, mais on pense qu'il a été réalisé aux environs du début des années 1780. La pièce est relativement simple, mais le choix de base du tempo dépend probablement du temps nécessaire à la transition entre la mesure 6 et la mesure 7.

Ferdinand Ries (1784– 1838)
18. Polonaise op. 124 no 3
($\downarrow$ = 96)

Publiée en 1832 dans le recueil de 15 pièces faciles pour le piano, la Polonaise de Ries contient des éléments caractéristiques de la période classique : motifs de gammes à la main droite, d'abord sur un balancement de croches à la main gauche, qui se transforme ensuite en un accompagnement en doubles croches (à partir de la mesure 15). Le f de la mesure 11 doit être très ferme à la fois dans l'articulation des doubles croches legato et dans celle des notes *staccato* de la basse.

Franz Schubert (1797–1828)
8. Ländler D 378 no 3
($\downarrow$. = 60)

Ce court *Ländler* est typique de la musique de ce style : deux parties de huit mesures chacune, fondées sur une séquence d'harmonies souvent prévisibles. L'art de Schubert, si ce n'est son génie, fut d'utiliser ces motifs pour en créer des œuvres dont la variété mélodique semble illimitée. Dans le cas de cette danse, la main droite doit être articulée par groupes de deux croches, qu'elles soient legato ou staccato. Dans la seconde partie, vous pouvez donner moins de poids aux blanches pointées la première fois et les souligner lors de la reprise.

Georg Christoph Wagenseil (1715–1777)
1. Allegro, du Divertimento no 2
($\downarrow$. = 66–72)

Cet allegro est une pièce efficace pour l'apprentissage des niveaux dynamiques. Les indications de jeu sont entièrement de l'éditeur et, en tant que telles, arbitraires, mais elles vous permettront de souligner la nouveauté apportée par le pianoforte à cette époque par rapport au clavecin, c'est-à-dire la possibilité de jouer fortement et doucement par le biais d'un ajustement du toucher. Il est fort vraisemblable qu'au moment de sa composition, cette musique ait été jouée au clavecin, mais les goûts musicaux – et la facture instrumentale – changèrent dans les 15 à 20 années qui suivirent. Cette pièce de Wagenseil pourra être une bonne introduction à l'étude du *Scherzo* de Haydn dans la même tonalité (no 14 de ce recueil).

Carl Maria von Weber (1786–1826)

La pièce pour piano la plus célèbre de Weber, son *Invitation à la danse* op. 65, fut l'une des plus populaires du dix-neuvième siècle et celle qui jouit de la plus grande longévité. Objet d'innombrables « arrangements de concert » réalisés par différents pianistes virtuoses, elle lia le nom du compositeur avec la forme de danse en tant que genre. De manière quelque peu surprenante, les petites danses de Weber ne connurent jamais le même engouement, alors qu'il s'agit souvent de pièces intrinsèquement tout à fait attrayantes et efficaces. Les valses figurant dans cette anthologie datent toutes deux de 1812 et appartiennent à un ensemble de six valses composées à la demande de l'éditeur de musique A. Kühnel.

22. Favoritwaltzer J. 143–8 no 4
($\downarrow$ = 63)

Les notes répétées des mesures 5–6 sont un élément caractéristique de l'écriture de Weber pour le piano qu'il n'utilisait pas seulement dans ses œuvres de moindre envergure, mais aussi dans le répertoire de concert comme la sonate op. 24. Écoutez attentivement les croches aux deux mains, car elles doivent être assemblées avec beaucoup de précision. Les notes arpégées de la basse dans le *Trio* sont certainement un clin d'œil au *Rondo alla turca* de la dernière sonate pour piano KV 331 de Mozart !

23. Favoritwaltzer J. 143–8 no 2
($\downarrow$ = 58)

C'est peut-être un avis très personnel, mais si le charme et la tragédie pouvaient coexister en une même page, ce serait certainement celle-ci. La *Valse* et le *Trio* s'articulent tous deux en une première partie d'humeur légère et une seconde plus dramatique. L'ornement de la mesure 12 peut être joué sur le dernier temps de la mesure, comme un groupe de quatre doubles-croches.

Samuel Wesley (1766– 1837)
6. Vivace de la Sonatine op. 12 no 8
(♩ = 88)
Seule la liaison de la mesure 4 est présente dans l'édition de 1799 (environ). Toutes les autres indications de jeu sont de l'éditeur. Pour les besoins de cet enregistrement, j'ai décidé de jouer les doubles croches de deux manières différentes afin de créer une variété dans le toucher : elles sont *staccato* mesures 1–8 et 17–24, détachées mesures 9–16. Mais il s'agit uniquement d'une suggestion. La partition a délibérément été laissée vierge de toute indication de jeu afin que vous puissiez y noter les vôtres. Aux mesures 9–14, tous les motifs de doubles croches suivis d'une croche couvrent une séquence de cinq notes, d'où le doigté suggéré. Encore une fois, si l'un des doigtés proposés ne vous semble pas confortable à votre main, modifiez-le.

Notes biographiques

Johann Christoph Friedrich Bach (1732–1795)
Johann Christoph Friedrich Bach apprit la musique auprès de son père, Jean-Sébastien, tout en fréquentant la *Thomasschule* à Leipzig. Il fut ensuite employé en tant que claveciniste à Bückeburg, dans une région qui joua un rôle important tout au long de sa vie. En 1759, il était *Kappellmeister* de l'orchestre de la cour locale. En 1778, il demanda la permission de rendre visite à son frère Johann Christian Bach à Londres, où il publia six concertos pour instrument à clavier et une série de quatuors à cordes. Il revint de Londres en rapportant un pianoforte anglais et il est vraisemblable, sinon certain, que la musique pour instrument à clavier qu'il a écrite par la suite est destinée à cet instrument plutôt qu'au clavecin. Bach fut également un professeur très apprécié et compta parmi ses élèves le futur élève de Mozart et *Thomaskantor* August Eberhard Müller (voir chez Schott, *Anthologie du piano classique* vol. 1).

Ludwig van Beethoven (1770–1827)
L'influence de Beethoven sur la musique de son temps ainsi que sur le développement des compositeurs de la génération suivante a été considérable et multiple. Son propre développement stylistique en tant que compositeur débouche sur un classement de sa production en trois périodes distinctes : jusqu'à environ 1802 (première période), de 1802 à 1812 (période intermédiaire) et à partir de 1812 (période tardive). En termes d'écriture pianistique, ces périodes reflètent l'héritage classique de la phase initiale, le développement de son style virtuose au clavier et l'individualité structurelle et technique qui en a découlé dans ses œuvres plus tardives.

En tant que compositeur, Beethoven excellait dans presque toutes les formes de musique instrumentale, du quatuor à cordes et de la sonate pour piano au concerto et à la symphonie. La spontanéité, la force et l'impact émotionnel de sa musique sont cependant le résultat d'un processus de composition méticuleux, documenté en détail grâce à ses carnets d'esquisses et ses manuscrits. Beethoven était un pianiste-interprète reconnu, bien que les témoignages contemporains sur sa façon de jouer diffèrent selon le point de vue de leur auteur. Tandis que certains louent sa puissance et la projection du son, d'autres trouvent son jeu brouillon et manquant de contrôle. Cependant, l'impact du jeu de Beethoven sur ses auditeurs est un point sur lequel la plupart des sources sont d'accord.

La fantaisie pour piano op. 77 est une œuvre pour piano où ces deux perspectives de son jeu sont réunies. Souvent considérée comme la version écrite d'une improvisation, elle contient de nombreux éléments caractéristiques de l'écriture de Beethoven du point de vue de l'harmonie, de la mélodie et de la texture, et en tant que telle, offre un aperçu unique des mécanismes d'écriture de ce grand musicien.

Les réalisations musicales de Beethoven sont si considérables que les générations suivantes de compositeurs, de Schubert à Schumann, Liszt et Brahms ont hésité un certain temps avant d'écrire dans un genre que Beethoven s'était approprié avant eux.

Domenico Cimarosa (1749–1801)
Cimarosa doit sa célébrité actuelle essentiellement à ses opéras. Après une formation de chant, violon et instruments à clavier dans sa Naples natale, la popularité grandissante de ses opéras lui permit de quitter Naples pour Venise, puis pour la cour de Russie à Saint-Pétersbourg où il travailla de 1787 à 1791. Il se rendit ensuite à Vienne avant de retourner à Naples en 1793. Ses opinions pro-républicaines lui valurent quelques problèmes dans l'Italie mouvante des années 1790 et, après un bref emprisonnement en 1799, il retourna à Venise où il mourut en 1801.

Les œuvres scéniques de Cimarosa était tenues en haute estime par nombre de ses contemporains. On sait que Haydn dirigea plusieurs de ses opéras, mais la réception de ses œuvres pour instruments à clavier est moins documentée. La plupart de ses sonates pour clavier comportent un mouvement unique et utilisent souvent la forme binaire. Bien que leur matériau mélodique les situe clairement dans la période classique, leur style transparent allié à leur format structurel invite à les comparer aux sonates pour clavier de Scarlatti.

Muzio Clementi (1752–1832)
Clementi naquit à Rome, mais s'installa en Angleterre en 1766 à l'initiative de Peter Beckford (1740–1792) dont il occupa le domaine du Dorset pour les sept années suivantes. En 1774, Clementi partit vivre à Londres avant de commencer une tournée de concerts sur le continent en 1780. En 1782, dans une lettre adressée à son père, Mozart critiquait le jeu de Clementi qu'il jugeait trop mécanique, malgré son admiration pour son jeu de tierces. En 1785, Clementi retourna à Londres où il resta jusqu'en 1802 et diversifia ses activités, exerçant à la fois en tant que professeur, concertiste, éditeur, chef d'orchestre et facteur de pianos. La vie de Clementi se poursuivit en un mélange de ces diverses activités musicales (y compris des tournées à l'étranger), sur lesquelles ses affaires commerciales finirent par prendre progressivement le pas. Il prit sa retraite en 1830.

Clementi eut pour élèves un grand nombre de pianistes-compositeurs célèbres comme Johann-Baptist Cramer, John Field ou Frederic Kalkbrenner. Sa compréhension du développement de l'art pianistique et la contribution qu'il y apporta apparaissent clairement dans deux publications importantes : un ouvrage pédagogique intitulé *Introduction to the Art of Playing on the Piano Forte* (ou *Introduction à l'art de jouer du pianoforte*) et un recueil de pièces destinées à promouvoir une évolution de l'art pianistique intitulé *Gradus at Parnassum*.

Johann Baptist Cramer (1771–1858)
Né en Allemagne, Cramer émigra en Angleterre à l'âge de trois ans avec sa famille. En 1783, il étudia pendant un an avec Muzio Clementi dont le style pianistique exerça sur lui une influence majeure lorsqu'il développa son propre style. Le *legato* de Cramer le rendit d'ailleurs célèbre parmi ses collègues et ses auditeurs. Comme Clementi avant lui, Cramer s'arrangea pour allier une carrière d'interprète, de professeur et d'homme d'affaires, s'impliquant dans l'édition musicale à partir de 1805. Ces rôles en apparence

différents n'étaient pas rares parmi les musiciens de la seconde moitié du 18e siècle, en particulier dans la mesure où l'écriture et la publication de matériel pédagogique constituaient un marché relativement lucratif. Ses *84 Études pour le piano* (publiées en 1804 et 1810 en deux groupes de 42 études) étaient destinées à un public d'élèves pianistes et furent autant un succès commercial qu'elles eurent d'influence d'un point de vue pianistique. Beethoven les recommandait pour le développement d'une bonne technique pianistique (il annota des études choisies de Cramer, mettant en valeur leurs objectifs musicaux individuels), Schumann les utilisa, Hanselt composa une seconde partie de piano pour l'y adjoindre et Carl Tausig (l'un des pianistes les plus célèbres du 19e siècle, élève de Liszt) édita une sélection de ces études soulignant ainsi leur pertinence presque un demi siècle après leur première publication. Avant 1800, la vie de Cramer semble avoir consisté en leçons de piano et en tournées européennes. Après cette date, il resta essentiellement en Angleterre, se concentrant sur ses l'édition musicale et sur la composition. À son départ à la retraite en 1835, il était un membre hautement respecté de la vie musicale londonienne.

Carl Czerny (1791–1857)

Czerny fut et demeure une figure significative du développement de l'art pianistique. Bien que sa mémoire soit surtout associée à Beethoven pour avoir été son élève, ainsi qu'à Liszt pour avoir été son professeur, Carl Czerny est un compositeur intéressant pour lui-même. Cependant, l'approche systématique qu'il appliqua au développement de ses propres recueils d'exercices pour le piano étant identique à la façon méticuleuse dont il documenta ses cours avec Beethoven et ses premières impressions de Liszt, il n'est pas surprenant qu'on se souvienne davantage de lui dans ce contexte.

Deux œuvres de jeunesse de Czerny, sa sonate pour piano op. 7 (interprétée par Liszt à Paris en 1830) et sa symphonie très dramatique en ut mineur, sont peut-être les meilleurs témoins de ses dons personnels en tant que compositeur. À l'âge de 16 ans, il décida de ne pas poursuivre sa carrière de concertiste, mais de se consacrer en lieu et place à l'enseignement. C'est ce qu'il fit, travaillant souvent dix heures et plus par jour, jusqu'à sa retraite en 1836.

Parmi tous les pianistes de son temps, Czerny est sans conteste celui qui laissa l'héritage pédagogique le plus exhaustif, comme en témoigne sa *Pianoforte-Schule* op. 500, ouvrage qu'il mit à jour en 1846.

Carl Ditters von Dittersdorf (1739–1799)

À l'heure actuelle, Dittersdorf, violoniste et compositeur autrichien, est moins connu pour ses compositions pour le clavier que pour les autres. Son œuvre prolifique comprend des oratorios, des symphonies, de la musique de chambre, recouvrant presque tous les genres avec lesquels il entra en contact. Cela tient sans doute à ses fonctions de *Kappellmeister* et d'impresario. En 1763, Dittersdorf fit une tournée en tant que violoniste avec Gluck en Italie, avant d'accepter le poste de *Kappellmeister* auprès de l'évêque de Grosswardein, où il succéda à Michael Haydn (frère de Joseph Haydn). Après une période d'incertitude politique dans les années 1770, Dittersdorf connut à nouveau le succès à Vienne pendant la seconde moitié des années 1780, période au cours de laquelle il se rendit également à Berlin pour interpréter ses œuvres.

La musique de Dittersdorf connut une popularité considérable, à tel point qu'il reste parfois difficile de vérifier l'authenticité de certaines de ses œuvres.

Johann Wilhelm Hässler (1747–1822)

Né à Erfurt en 1747, Hässler se forma auprès de son oncle, Johann Christian Kittel, organiste dans cette ville. À l'âge de 16 ans, il fut engagé pour la première fois en tant qu'organiste à Erfurt, mais commença bientôt à voyager dans toute l'Allemagne en tant que concertiste. Il fonda sa propre maison d'édition en 1780. En 1790, il avait voyagé aussi loin que l'Angleterre et la Russie, où il devint chef d'orchestre à la cour de Saint-Pétersbourg en 1792. Dans une lettre de 1788, le poète et écrivain Friedrich von Schiller se souvient des prestations de Hässler : « Il joue comme un maître et compose très bien. En tant que personne, c'est un original au tempérament plutôt fougueux. »[1] À partir de 1794, Hässler vécut à Moscou ou il exerça en tant que professeur de piano très respecté et recherché. Sa contribution au développement du pianisme russe au cours de la première moitié du 19e siècle reste à déterminer, mais la plupart de ses œuvres pour piano publiées suggèrent clairement qu'il s'intéressait au développement des capacités d'instrumentistes peu expérimentés.

Le style personnel de Hässler au clavier s'est développé à partir de l'écriture pianistique de C.P.E. Bach, mais partage son accessibilité avec les premières sonates pour piano de Haydn. Parmi ses petites pièces pédagogiques et ses sonates pour piano faciles, nombreuses sont celles qui bénéficient d'un attrait musical immédiat et sa méthode pour piano contient un grand nombre d'œuvres encore exploitables aujourd'hui.

Joseph Haydn (1732–1809)

L'estimation de la place de Haydn en tant que compositeur a été soumise à de nombreuses variations avec le temps. La perception populaire de sa vie se focalise souvent sur le relatif confort et la stabilité de ses presque 30 ans d'engagement auprès de la famille Esterhazy à Eisenstadt, près de Vienne. Malgré une existence effectivement relativement sédentaire (du moins par rapport à nombre de ses contemporains, et notamment à Mozart), la musique de Haydn fut largement publiée après 1780, lui permettant ainsi de jouir d'une réputation nationale et internationale croissante. À partir de 1791, ses visites à Londres vinrent confirmer ses succès économiques et musicaux.

Pourtant, ses premières années avaient été très différentes. Après une formation initiale de choriste et de violoniste, Haydn, qui n'était pas un virtuose, survécut en donnant des cours et en intégrant des ensembles jouant de la musique fonctionnelle. Du point de vue de la composition, essentiellement autodidacte, il progressa lentement jusqu'à acquérir les compétences nécessaires qui lui permirent, à partir du milieu des années 1760, de développer un style musical plus caractéristique.

La production pour piano de Haydn comprend plus de 60 sonates, pièces individuelles et variations. Bien que n'étant pas virtuose, il savait exactement comment écrire efficacement pour le pianoforte. Toutes ses œuvres viennent très bien sous les doigts (quel que soit leur degré de complexité), mais c'est l'élément de surprise, à la fois en termes d'harmonie et de texture pianistique, qui donne leur charme particulier à nombre de ses compositions. L'écriture pianistique de Haydn n'obéit jamais à des formules et garde ainsi toujours un caractère légèrement imprévisible.

James Hook (1746–1827)

Il semble que le talent musical de Hook se révéla très tôt dans sa vie. Il donna des concerts publics dès l'âge de six ans et aurait composé ses premières œuvres d'envergure à huit ans, même si

1) Kahl, W., *Selbstbiographien Deutscher Musiker* (Koeln und Krefeld, Staufen Verlag, 1948), p. 47

celles-ci sont aujourd'hui considérées comme perdues.

Après s'être installé à Londres en 1764, Hook occupa successivement plusieurs postes en tant qu'organiste dans la région londonienne, composant de la musique vocale, dont des opéras, et enseignant les instruments à clavier à titre privé, activité dans laquelle il était très demandé. Ses activités d'enseignant expliquent l'origine de la plus grande partie de ses œuvres pédagogiques pour le piano, qui sont à la fois élégantes et gratifiantes d'un point de vue technique. Les sonatines op. 12 furent publiées en 1775.

Johann Nepomuk Hummel (1778–1837)

Hummel fut indubitablement une figure charnière de son époque, tant du point de vue pianistique que de l'écriture. La musique de Hummel, qui fut l'élève de Mozart, conserva toujours ses racines classiques en termes de structure et de détail musical. Cependant, en tant que pianiste, et plus important sans doute, en tant que professeur de piano influent, Hummel forma de nombreux représentants de la première génération du pianisme du 19e siècle : Henselt, Hiller, Mendelssohn et Thalberg ont tous bénéficié de son enseignement. D'autres pianistes de cette époque ont également subi son influence. Schumann envisagea d'étudier avec lui et si, pour finir, il ne le fit pas, les figurations décoratives de Hummel à la main droite l'occupèrent clairement, comme en témoignent les *Variations Abegg* op. 1 ainsi que d'autres œuvres de jeunesse. Liszt entra lui aussi en contact avec la musique de Hummel en jouant ses concertos pour piano op. 85 et 89 au début de sa carrière de virtuose itinérant. Même Chopin fut sans doute familier de la musique de Hummel, car certaines de ses premières œuvres dénotent des similitudes stylistiques et parfois même mélodiques.

La méthode de piano parue 1828, un document de 450 pages qui prétend mener l'élève « de la première leçon à la formation la plus complète » constitue l'une des réalisations les plus remarquables de Hummel.[1] Publiée à Vienne par Tobias Haslinger (voir morceau no 10 de la présente anthologie), il s'agit peut-être de la première méthode complète pour piano du 19e siècle établissant les concepts techniques sur lesquels se fonde l'art pianistique virtuose de cette période. Hormis la méthodologie d'apprentissage approfondie de Hummel, le caractère remarquable de cette méthode réside dans la conscience de son auteur de notions pédagogiques et de ses réflexions s'y rapportant : interaction maître-élève, motivation et déroulement du cours sont parmi les sujets explorés par Hummel.

Wolfgang Amadeus Mozart (1756–1791)

Mozart naquit dans un environnement très musical. Son père Léopold était pédagogue et violoniste dans un orchestre à Salzbourg tandis que sa grande sœur, Nannerl, avait déjà révélé ses capacités au piano. Mozart fit des progrès rapides dans ses études musicales, à tel point que son père décida de l'emmener dans une tournée de concerts en l'Allemagne, puis à Londres et Paris. Ces voyages durèrent trois ans et demi avant que Mozart s'installe à Salzbourg en 1766. S'ensuivirent entre 1769 et 1772 des voyages annuels en Italie, qui permirent à Mozart d'entrer en contact avec de nombreux autres musiciens, comme il le fit tout au long de sa vie. Au début des années 1780, il semble que Mozart se soit établit comme musicien indépendant, avec tout ce que cela implique. Certains de ses concertos pour piano les plus célèbres datent de cette période, ainsi que nombre de ses quatuors à cordes dont il interpréta certain avec Joseph Haydn, leur dédicataire. À la fin de cette décennie (et au début de la suivante), Mozart rencontra

un succès considérable comme compositeur d'opéra, avec des œuvres comme *Cosi fan tutte* et *La flûte enchantée*.

La diversité de ses œuvres pour piano reflète naturellement les différentes périodes de la vie du compositeur. Certaines parmi les plus précoces ont été écrites alors qu'il était à peine âgé de 5 ans, une époque où il écrivait principalement de courtes danses. Les œuvres de sa maturité incluent sonates, variations et pièces individuelles écrites le plus souvent à son usage personnel.

Ferdinand Ries (1784–1838)

Ries reçut sa formation musicale initiale de son père, Franz Ries, qui lui enseigna le piano et le violon. Afin de financer la suite de ses études, Ferdinand travailla en 1801 comme copiste de musique à Munich avant de s'installer à Vienne un an plus tard. Il y étudia le piano avec Beethoven pendant trois ans et la composition avec Albrechtsberger. Beethoven apporta un soutien significatif à sa carrière de virtuose international et Ries se produisit dans toute l'Europe au cours des décennies suivantes. En 1813, il arriva à Londres où il resta 14 ans et épousa une Anglaise en 1814. La période anglaise de Ries semble avoir été la plus stable de sa vie, y compris du point de vue financier. À sa retraite en 1824, il retourna en Allemagne, d'abord à Godesberg, puis trois ans plus tard, à Francfort.

La musique de Ries conserve ses racines classiques à travers toutes ses créations. Son concerto pour piano en do dièse mineur op. 55 est son œuvre la plus célèbre pour le piano.

Franz Schubert (1797–1828)

La formation musicale initiale de Schubert lui a été prodiguée par son père et par ses frères qui lui enseignèrent le piano, le violon et l'alto. À l'âge de 11 ans, il bénéficia d'une bourse d'études qui lui permit de se former auprès de Salieri. Ensuite, à 16 ans, Schubert décida de se former à l'enseignement et commença un an plus tard à travailler dans l'école de son père. À 17 ans, il avait écrit certains de ses premiers chefs-d'œuvre, dont *Le Roi des aulnes et Marguerite au rouet*, pour voix et piano. En 1816, Schubert abandonna son poste d'enseignant et choisit de vivre au centre de Vienne et de se consacrer à la composition. S'ensuivit une période d'incertitude financière, mais à la fin de 1819, Schubert écrivit son premier chef-d'œuvre de musique de chambre, son quintette intitulé *La Truite*. Au printemps 1821, le succès du *Roi des aulnes* déboucha sur la publication de ses airs par Diabelli, qui lui permit de connaître une courte période de stabilité financière. De 1820 à 1823, il se lança dans l'écriture de musique d'opéra, une entreprise malheureusement peu fructueuse, pour finalement se tourner vers l'écriture de musique de chambre et de musique symphonique les trois dernières années de ma vie. À quelques rares exceptions près, l'écriture pianistique de Schubert ne se préoccupe pas d'effets techniques tels que le font certains de ses contemporains. Au contraire, toutes les exigences de sa musique proviennent de la prééminence du propos musical sur toute autre forme de considération pianistique.

Georg Christoph Wagenseil (1715–1777)

L'importance historique de Wagenseil trouve ses origines dans ses activités de compositeur et professeur à la cour d'Autriche. De par la polyvalence de ses aptitudes musicales, il marqua la génération suivante de compositeurs tels que J. A. Steffan (voir

---

1) Hummel, J. N., *Anweisung zum Piano-forte spielen* (Wien: Haslinger, 1828)

Schott *Anthologie du piano classique* Vol. 3) et F. X. Dusek, et influa largement sur la formation du style classique émergeant après 1750. Ses quatre recueils de divertimentos pour claviers op. 1 à 4 furent publiés entre 1753 et 1763 et connurent un succès immédiat. En 1762, à l'âge de six ans, le jeune Mozart joua l'un des concertos de Wagenseil en public, ce qui en dit long sur le succès de ce compositeur à cette époque. Il n'est donc pas surprenant que les premiers cahiers de Mozart présentent des similitudes de texture avec les œuvres pour clavier de Wagenseil. Cependant, le style de Wagenseil ne représentait pas uniquement une simple transition vers la période classique. L'élégance de sa musique était fondée sur la volonté d'écrire efficacement pour les élèves, ainsi qu'en témoigne sa position de *Hofklaviermeister* à partir de 1749.

Carl Maria von Weber (1786–1826)

La première partie de la vie de Weber est emblématique de celle de nombreux musiciens de son temps. Son éducation musicale lui fut prodiguée par son père et par plusieurs musiciens locaux. Ses voyages en Allemagne et en Autriche lui permirent ensuite de rencontrer Michael Haydn (frère de Joseph et compositeur très reconnu) ainsi que le compositeur et théoricien Georg Joseph Vogler qui lui dispensa une grande partie de l'enseignement systématique dont il avait besoin. Weber déménagea de ville en ville jusqu'en 1810, occupant successivement différents de postes musicaux, voire dans certains cas, administratifs. Une action en justice contre Weber et son père ainsi que leur arrestation et, pour finir, leur bannissement du land du Wurtemberg, eurent sur lui un profond retentissement. Déterminé à changer de vie, il passa les deux années suivantes à composer, donner des concerts et à vivre à la hauteur de ses moyens. Il fut bientôt engagé en tant que directeur musical à la cour et/ou au théâtre, d'abord à Prague entre 1813 et 1816 puis à Dresde entre 1817 et 1821, périodes au cours desquelles il continua également à voyager en tant qu'interprète. Le changement sans doute le plus important dans la vie de Weber fut provoqué par l'extraordinaire popularité de son opéra, *Der Freischütz* (1820), une œuvre qui assura son succès dans toute l'Allemagne ainsi qu'à l'étranger.

L'écriture pianistique de Weber est caractéristique, mais reste cependant difficile à résumer. Elle est clairement dominée par la mélodie, dans la mesure où elle est souvent homophonique, avec une attirance particulière pour les formes de danses et les motifs rythmiques pointés qui sous-tendent son style de composition. En tant que pianiste, Weber écrit souvent de manière élaborée et virtuose pour la main droite : des progressions d'accords rapides, des croisements de mains et des extensions dépassant largement la position d'une main. En ce sens, l'écriture pour piano de Weber est fondée sur la technique fluide de gammes et d'arpèges également privilégiée par Hummel, mais il occupe une position intermédiaire entre ce dernier et le discours pianistique de Chopin et Liszt à partir des années 1830.

Samuel Wesley (1766– 1837)

Samuel Wesley fut un personnage brillant, mais aussi controversé, de la vie musicale de son temps. Né à Bristol, il s'installa à Londres avec ses parents en 1771. La situation du domicile familial à Maribelone s'avéra être une excellente plateforme qui permit à Wesley de valoriser très tôt ses talents musicaux. La remarque de William Boyce en 1774, qui qualifiait le jeune musicien de « Mozart anglais », est révélatrice de ses succès précoces. Principalement organiste, Wesley mena une carrière professionnelle typique des musiciens de son temps, gagnant sa vie en tant que professeur, concertiste et compositeur. Malgré l'immense respect dont il bénéficiait pour ses activités musicales, le non-conformiste de sa vie privée et ses fréquentes périodes de dépression l'empêchèrent de trouver sa place au centre de la vie musicale anglaise. Malheureusement, une grande partie de sa musique pou clavier reste indisponible à l'heure actuelle, malgré un style accessible et la fraîcheur de son invention.

Nils Franke

Bibliographie

Hinson, Maurice.
Guide to the Pianist's Repertoire.
Bloomington and Indianapolis: Indiana University Press, 2000

MacGrath, Jane.
The Pianist's Guide to Standard Teaching and Performance Literature.
Van Nuys: Alfred Publishing Co., 1995

Prosnitz, Adolf.
Handbuch der Klavierliteratur.
Wien: Doblinger, 1908

Sadie, Stanley (ed.)
Grove Concise Dictionary of Music.
London: MacMillan Publishers, 1988

Sadie, Stanley (ed.)
Grove Dictionary of Music online.
[accessed 04/04/2011]

Wolters, Klaus.
Handbuch der Klavierliteratur zu zwei Händen.
Zürich and Mainz: Atlantis Musikbuch Verlag, 2001

Spielhinweise

Eine der interessanten Herausforderungen beim Spielen klassischer Musik ist der Umgang mit dem Unterschied zwischen dem Pianoforte des späten 18. Jahrhunderts und dem heutigen Klavier. Die Unterschiede sind zwar recht groß, doch können eingebrachte Kenntnisse über die damaligen Instrumente unseren Umgang mit der Musik bereichern, auch wenn wir sie auf modernen Instrumenten spielen. So hatte das Klavier der Klassik leichtere (und weniger) Tasten, die Saiten verliefen parallel zueinander, d.h. es gab keine kreuzsaitige Bespannung, die Hämmer waren nicht mit Filz, sondern mit Leder bezogen, es war insgesamt zierlicher, hatte keinen Metallrahmen und eine andere Mechanik. All das bedeutet, dass wir den Klang, den Haydn oder Mozart hörten, nicht reproduzieren können. Wir können das moderne Klavier jedoch so spielen, dass es diesen anderen musikalischen Gegebenheiten gerecht wird. Um dies zu erreichen, sollte man mit starken dynamischen Kontrasten zwischen *forte* und *piano* arbeiten und das rechte Pedal so einsetzen, dass es nur bestimmte Stellen der Musik hervorhebt und nicht allgegenwärtig ist. Die Klangqualität sollte sich grundsätzlich eher an den Höhen als an den Bässen des Instruments orientieren. Verzierungen sind ebenfalls wichtig, und die CD enthält hin und wieder Verzierungen an Stellen, an denen Kadenzen vorkommen. Die Verwendung von Verzierungen ist häufig eine Frage der persönlichen Entscheidung. Am besten betrachtet man Verzierungen als Bereicherung einer Melodie.

Letztendlich bildet das Konzept der historisch geprägten Spielpraxis (d.h. ein Verständnis dafür, wie Musik in einer anderen Epoche gespielt wurde sowie der Einfluss dessen auf das eigene Spiel) eine hervorragende Grundlage für das Experimentieren mit Musik sowie für die Fähigkeit zuzuhören, zu bewerten und musikalische Entscheidungen zu treffen.

Johann Christoph Friedrich Bach (1732–1795)
15. Solfeggio
($\quad = 52$)
Der Begriff *Solfeggio* bedeutet in diesem Zusammenhang Übung bzw. Etüde. Es ist offensichtlich, was Bach mit diesem Stück im Sinn hatte: eine Gleichmäßigkeitsübung, sowohl für das Tempo als auch für den Anschlag. Darüber hinaus kann das Stück auch als Kompositionsübung betrachtet werden, da jeder halbe Takt (bzw. in Takt 5–6 jeder Viertelschlag) aus einem Akkord besteht. Beim Erlernen des Stückes kann es nützlich sein, zuerst Bachs Akkordfolge zu lernen, bevor man das Stück wie notiert spielt. Die Inspiration zu diesem Werk lieferte wahrscheinlich das Präludium BWV846 von Bachs Vater.

Ludwig van Beethoven (1770–1827)
9. Ländlerischer Tanz, WoO 11 Nr. 2
($\quad = 60$)
Dieser Tanz stammt aus einer Sammlung mit sieben Stücken, die 1799 veröffentlicht wurden. Der Tanzcharakter wird zweifellos durch die Staccatonoten in der rechten Hand verstärkt. Der Mittelteil erfordert jedoch einen anderen Anschlag, und das Stück lebt von den verschiedenen Artikulationsformen. Bereits am Anfang muss sich die staccato gespielte Melodie deutlich von der nicht staccato gespielten Begleitung abheben. Dies ist zwar zunächst nicht ganz einfach, es lohnt sich jedoch, daran zu arbeiten.

25. Klavierstück, WoO54 „Lustig-traurig"
($\quad = 60$)
Der Untertitel dieses Klavierstückes, „lustig und traurig", cha-

rakterisiert die Musik und unterstreicht somit die unterschiedlichen Stimmungen in der Dur- und Molltonart. Um dem Werk Einheitlichkeit zu verleihen, sollte es in einem Tempo gespielt werden, das für beide Teile angemessen ist. Im Mollteil besteht die Herausforderung in der Einheitlichkeit beider Hände, während es im Durteil um das sorgfältige Voicing der Akkordfolgen geht. Außerdem sollte Beethovens Phrasierung beachtet werden, da sie die Musik in abgeschlossene Einheiten aufteilt – ähnlich wie beim Sprechen.

Domenico Cimarosa (1749–1801)
2. Sonata
($\quad = 60$)
Hier wird häufig das Stilmittel der Wiederholung zwei- bzw. viertaktiger Phrasen eingesetzt, die jedoch mit einem dynamischen Wechsel oder einer anderen Artikulation verbunden ist. Somit kommen oft Wechsel zwischen f und p vor, es gibt jedoch auch Gelegenheiten, um mit dem Anschlag zu experimentieren. In Takt 13 und 14 könnte man z.B. mit der linken Hand die erste Achtel im Takt zum nächsten Takt überbinden und so einen tänzerischen 3/4-Rhythmus erzeugen. Obwohl es so nicht notiert ist, passt es hervorragend zu diesem eleganten und reizvollen Stück.

Muzio Clementi (1752–1832)
17. Arietta
($\quad = 60$)
Dieses Stück ist die Klavierlektion Nr. 22 aus Clementis Klavierlehrbuch, das sowohl Eigenkompositionen als auch Werke anderer Komponisten enthält. Es gewährt einen faszinierenden Einblick in das Unterrichtsrepertoire des 18. Jahrhunderts, und es ist interessant zu lesen, welche pianistischen Fähigkeiten Clementi für wichtig erachtet, und in welcher Reihenfolge sie erlernt werden sollen. Im vorliegenden Stück geht es um die Koordination von Achteln und Sechzehnteln, wobei Letztere eine stützende Funktion haben und daher leiser gespielt werden. Die Kadenz in Takt 16 ist eine wichtige Stelle, und die Fermate (Pause) zeigt an, dass es sich um eine improvisatorische Stelle handelt. Allerdings sollte die vom Komponisten vorgenommene Aufteilung der folgenden Noten in Zweiunddreißigstel, Sechzehntel und Achtel nicht so sehr als einschränkende Notation empfunden werden, sondern eher als ein ausnotiertes, deutlich sichtbar gemachtes Ritardando. Die Verzierung in Takt 2 und 18 kann in Form von vier Zweiunddreißigsteln gespielt werden, die auf H beginnen und dem Rhythmus der entsprechenden Noten in der linken Hand angepasst werden.

Johann Baptist Cramer (1771–1858)
5. Guaracha
($\quad = 76$)
Aus Cramers Anmerkungen zu diesem Stück geht hervor, dass er Wert auf eine leichte Betonung der Eins jedes Taktes legt, wahrscheinlich um den tänzerischen Charakter dieses spanischen Tanzes hervorzuheben. Diese betonten Noten helfen bei der Koordination der Sechzehntel in der rechten Hand ab Takt 9.

10. Präludium & Andantino
($\quad = 88$) ($\quad = 52$)
Damals war es durchaus üblich, dem Hauptstück, in diesem Fall dem *Andantino*, eine musikalische Einleitung voranzustellen. Diese diente mehreren Zwecken: Der Interpret konnte sich auf das konzentrieren, was gleich kommen würde, die Zuhörer wurden auf die Tonart vorbereitet, und der Komponist konnte entweder den Charakter des folgenden Stückes vorstellen oder einen Kontrast dazu

bilden. Letzteres macht Cramer hier: Die rege Einleitung mündet hier nicht in ein Stück gleichen Charakters – vielmehr wirkt der Beginn des *Andantinos* auf die Zuhörer etwas überraschend.

Carl Czerny (1791–1857)

13. Andante op. 453 No. 32
(♩. = 80)
19. Andantino op. 453 No. 41
(♩. = 76)

Hier sind beide Stücke von Czerny enthalten, und zwar nicht aus irgendwelchen technischen Gründen, sondern wegen ihres musikalischen Reizes. Ein Vergleich beider Stücke zeigt jedoch zwei unterschiedliche Ansätze, eine Akkordgrundlage am Klavier zu erzeugen. Das *Andante* enthält einen gebrochenen Akkord, der in Verbindung mit dem Pedaleinsatz der Melodie als Stütze dient. Im *Andantino* erfordert der gehaltene Basston einen sorgfältigeren Pedaleinsatz, damit drei Stimmen (Bass-, Ober- und Mittelstimme) zu hören sind.

Carl Ditters von Dittersdorf (1739–1799)

4. Englischer Tanz Nr. 15
(♩ = 96)

Dieses Stück ist fast eine Miniatursuite aus Tänzen, die alle miteinander kombiniert wurden, um ein Ganzes zu bilden. Der Hauptteil ist der technisch schwierige Abschnitt. In Takt 9 und 11 kann man das rechte Pedal betätigen, um den Akkordklang zu halten, während die linke Hand zur darauf folgenden Terz wechselt. Am meisten Beachtung erfordern jedoch die Terzen in Takt 15. Hier kann man den Fingersatz wählen, und es ist ratsam, beide Fingersätze auszuprobieren, um herauszufinden, welcher besser funktioniert. Wenn die Terzen jedoch schwierig zu spielen sind, ist hier eine Alternative, die ähnlich klingt, sich aber vielleicht bequemer spielen lässt:

Johann Wilhelm Häßler (1747–1822)

11. Allegro assai op. 38 Nr. 20
(♩ = 104)
12. Presto op. 38 Nr. 29
(♩ = 86)

Beide Stücke stammen aus einer Sammlung mit kurzen Etüden, von denen jede eine andere technische Herausforderung enthält. In Nr. 20 geht es um die Arbeit mit beidhändigen Sechzehntelpassagen. Nr. 29 hat eher Improvisationscharakter und erinnert stark an ein romantisches Klavierpräludium, obwohl das Stück musikalisch weniger geschlossen ist als Nr. 20. Die Betonung der plötzlichen dynamischen Wechsel zwischen *f* und *p* reiht es eindeutig in den klassischen Kontext ein. Beide Stücke eignen sich gut zum Einspielen und Üben, da sie auch dann noch effektiv sind, wenn sie etwas langsamer gespielt werden.

Joseph Haydn (1732–1809)

14. Scherzo Hob. XVI:9
(♩ = 112)

Dieses *Scherzo* ist der letzte Satz einer frühen Klaviersonate, die vermutlich vor 1766 entstand. Schüler, die eine ganze Sonate ler-

nen und/oder vorspielen möchten, können das Stück als Ganzes angehen. Im *Allegro* ist allerdings die Spannweite einer Oktave für den Großteil der Stimme für die linke Hand wichtig. (Für eine vollständige Ausgabe der anderen Sätze s. Schott ED 9026.) Abgesehen von seinem einprägsamen Thema liegt der Reiz des *Scherzos* darin, dass beide Hände für die damalige Zeit typische Stilmittel spielen: Tonleitern und Arpeggien in der rechten Hand und Akkorde als harmonische Stütze in der linken.

24. Adagio Hob. XVII:9
(♪ = 98)

Das *Adagio* gehört zu einer Gruppe aus 10 kleinen Klavierstücken, die um 1786 veröffentlicht wurden. Alle zehn sind Transkriptionen von Haydns Noten, doch nur zwei, darunter das *Adagio*, sind als Manuskripte erhalten, die vom Komponisten geschrieben wurden. Am besten zählt man in Achteln, was auch die Tempoangabe am Anfang erklärt, weil sich Viertel sehr langsam anfühlen. Da genaue Spielanweisungen des Komponisten fehlen, sind Schüler und Lehrer bei diesem Stück recht flexibel und haben somit ein schönes Stück, um mit der Musik der Klassik zu experimentieren.

James Hook (1746–1827)

3. Rondo: Allegretto, aus Sonatina op. 12 Nr. 9
(♩ = 88)

Ein Rondo enthält ein zentrales Motiv, das immer wiederkehrt, jedoch mit anderen musikalischen Bestandteilen durchsetzt ist. Hooks Stück ist zwar genauso aufgebaut, jedoch stark verdichtet. Das zentrale Motiv (A) ist in Takt 1–8 zu finden. Es kehrt in Takt 17 und als *da capo* wieder. Die anderen Bestandteile sind in Takt 9–16 (B) und Takt 25–32 (C) zu finden. Insgesamt verleiht dies dem Stück den Aufbau ABACA. Wie bei Wiederholungen üblich kann man entscheiden, ob man etwas auf andere Weise oder absichtlich genauso spielen möchte. Wie die Entscheidung auch ausfällt: Sie ist immer das Ergebnis der Experimente mit Artikulation und Dynamik. Noten mit relativ wenigen Angaben erfordern die Mitwirkung des Interpreten!

Johann Nepomuk Hummel (1778–1837)

7. Allegro
(♩ = 104)

Hummel schrieb dieses Stück ausdrücklich für seine *Pianoforte-Schule* (1828) als musikalischen Rahmen für eine pianistische Fähigkeit, die erlernt werden sollte: das gleichmäßige Spiel von Sechzehntelpassagen. Zu diesem Zweck verwendet der Komponist in Takt 15–16 Akkorde und deren Umkehrungen, die den bisherigen Ablauf des Stückes unterbrechen. Im vorgeschlagenen Tempo können die Basstöne eine Melodie bilden, die das Stück allmählich zum Abschluss bringt.

20. Romanze op. 52 Nr. 4
(♩ = 84)

Hummels *6 leichte Klavierstücke* op. 52 sind eine Sammlung, die hauptsächlich für Klavierschüler geschrieben wurde. Nr. 5, *Eccosaise*, ist das leichteste Stück daraus und ist in der *Classical Piano Anthology Bd. 1* enthalten. Die übrigen Stücke haben den Schwierigkeitsgrad 4 bis 5, was die Sammlung insgesamt sehr nützlich für den Unterricht macht. Die *Romanze* ist das einzige lyrische Werk der Sammlung. Wie Clementis *Arietta* (Nr. 17 in diesem Buch) enthält Hummels Stück eine Kadenz vor der Rückkehr zum Hauptthema in Takt 21.

21. Gigue
(♩. = 98)

Obwohl die *Gigue* hauptsächlich mit der Barockmusik assoziiert wird, taucht dieser Tanz auch noch in der Musik klassischer Komponisten wie Mozart oder Hummel auf. Das Tempo des Werks muss so gewählt werden, dass man die vier Schläge pro Takt deutlich spürt. Aus spieltechnischer Sicht kann höchstens die zweistimmige Passage im letzten Takt ein paar Probleme bereiten. Wenn sich der Fingersatz des Komponisten als schwierig erweist, kann man folgende Aufteilung der Noten auf beide Hände ausprobieren:

Wolfgang Amadeus Mozart (1756–1791)
16. Tempo di Minuetto KV236
(♩ = 98)

Als dieses Werk Mitte des 19. Jahrhunderts erstmals veröffentlicht wurde, nahm man an, es sei eine Originalkomposition von Mozart. Aufgrund neuerer Forschungsergebnisse weiß man jedoch, dass es sich um die Klavierversion (von Mozart) einer Melodie von Christoph Willibald Gluck (1714–1787) handelt. Über die Datierung von Mozarts Bearbeitung herrscht zwar Uneinigkeit, doch entstand sie vermutlich Anfang der 1780er-Jahre. Das Stück ist relativ unkompliziert, doch hängt das Tempo wahrscheinlich von der Zeit ab, die man zum Übergang von Takt 6 zu Takt 7 benötigt.

Ferdinand Ries (1784–1838)
18. Polonaise op. 124 Nr. 3
(♩ = 96)

Ries *Polonaise* wurde 1832 in seinen *15 leichten Klavierstücken* veröffentlicht und enthält klassische Merkmale wie aus dem Lehrbuch: Tonleitern in der rechten Hand und zu Beginn eine wiegende Achtelsequenz in der linken, die später (ab Takt 15) in eine Sechzehntelbegleitung übergeht. Das *f* in Takt 11 muss sowohl bei den legato gespielten Sechzehnteln als auch bei den staccato gespielten Basstönen deutlich gespielt werden.

Franz Schubert (1797–1828)
8. Ländler D 378 Nr. 3
(♩. = 60)

Dieser kurze *Ländler* ist typisch für diesen Musikstil. Zweimal acht Takte mit einer oft vorhersagbaren Akkordfolge. Schuberts Fähigkeit, wenn nicht sogar Genialität, lag darin, aus diesen Merkmalen Werke mit einer scheinbar grenzenlosen melodischen Vielfalt zu komponieren. Bei diesem Tanz muss die Stimme für die rechte Hand in Gruppen aus zwei Achteln –ob staccato oder legato – artikuliert werden. Bei der Wiederholung der zweiten Hälfte können die punktierten Halben stärker betont werden als im ersten Durchgang.

Georg Christoph Wagenseil (1715–1777)
1. Allegro, aus Divertimento Nr. 2
(♩. = 66–72)

Dieses *Allegro* ist ein effektives Stück zum Erlernen der abgestuften Dynamik. Alle Spielanweisungen wurden vom Herausgeber hinzugefügt und sind daher Ermessenssache. Allerdings heben sie hervor, was damals am Pianoforte neu war und im Gegensatz zum Cembalo stand: die Möglichkeit, durch eine Veränderung des Anschlags laut und leise zu spielen. Wahrscheinlich wurde das Stück zur Zeit seiner Entstehung noch auf dem Cembalo gespielt, doch nur ca. 15 bis 20 Jahre später veränderte sich der Musikgeschmack (und der Instrumentenbau).

Dieses Stück von Wagenseil kann als nützliche Vorübung zu Haydns *Scherzo* (Nr. 14 dieser Anthologie) in derselben Tonart dienen.

Carl Maria von Weber (1786–1826)

Webers erfolgreichstes Klavierstück, *Aufforderung zum Tanz* op. 65, war im 19. Jahrhundert eines der beliebtesten und langlebigsten Klavierstücke. Es wurde von verschiedenen Klaviervirtuosen für Orchester bearbeitet und verband den Namen des Komponisten mit der Tanzform als Genre. Merkwürdigerweise fanden Webers kleine Tanzstücke nie dieselbe Beachtung, obgleich viele von ihnen durchaus wirkungsvoll sind. Die zwei Walzer in dieser Anthologie entstanden 1812 und gehören zu den sechs Walzern, die auf Wunsch des Musikverlegers A. Kühnel geschrieben wurden.

22. Favoritwalzer J. 143–8 Nr. 4
(♩. = 63)

Die wiederkehrenden Noten in Takt 5–6 sind typisch für Webers Klavierkompositionen. Er verwendete sie nicht nur in seinen kleineren Werken, sondern auch in seinen Konzertstücken, z.B. in der Klaviersonate op. 24. Man sollte sich die Achtel in beiden Händen aufmerksam anhören, da sie exakt zusammenklingen müssen. Die arpeggierten Basstöne im Trio verweisen höchstwahrscheinlich auf Mozarts *Rondo alla turca* (*Türkischer Marsch*) in dessen Klaviersonate KV 331!

23. Favoritwalzer J. 143–8 Nr. 2
(♩. = 58)

Auch wenn es meine ganz persönliche Ansicht ist: Wenn Anmut und Drama auf einer Seite miteinander kombiniert werden könnten, so wäre es in diesem Stück. Sowohl Walzer als auch *Trio* bestehen aus einem fröhlichen ersten und einem eher dramatischen zweiten Teil. Die Verzierung in Takt 12 kann als Gruppe aus vier Sechzehnteln auf dem letzten Taktschlag gespielt werden.

Samuel Wesley (1766–1837)
6. Vivace, aus Sonatina op. 12 Nr. 8
(♩ = 88)

Lediglich der Bindebogen in Takt 4 ist in der Werkausgabe von ca. 1799 angegeben; alle anderen Spielanweisungen wurden nachträglich hinzugefügt. Bei der CD-Aufnahme habe ich die Sechzehntel des Stückes auf zwei unterschiedliche Weisen gespielt, um dem Anschlag Abwechslung zu verleihen: Die Takte 1–8 und 17–24 werden *staccato* und die Takte 9–16 als *Non legato* gespielt. Dies ist jedoch lediglich ein Vorschlag. Die Noten enthalten absichtlich keine Spielanweisungen, damit die Interpreten ihre eigenen hineinschreiben können. In Takt 9–14 bestehen alle Sechzehntelpassagen, auf die eine Achtel folgt, aus fünf Tönen – daher der von mir vorgeschlagene Fingersatz. Auch hier gilt wieder: Wenn eine vorgeschlagene Spieltechnik nicht angenehm für die Hand ist, sollte man sie ändern.

Biografische Anmerkungen

Johann Christoph Friedrich Bach (1732–1795)

Johann Christoph Friedrich Bach wurde von seinem Vater Johann Sebastian unterrichtet, als er die Thomasschule in Leipzig besuchte. Anschließend wurde er in Bückeburg, einer Region, die zeit seines Lebens eine wichtige Rolle für ihn spielen würde, zum Hof-Cembalisten ernannt. 1759 wurde J. C. Bach zum Hofkapellmeister ernannt. 1778 ersuchte er um die Genehmigung, seinen Bruder Johann Christian Bach in London zu besuchen, wo er sechs Klavierkonzerte und einige Streichquartette veröffentlichte. Aus London kehrte er mit einem englischen Fortepiano zurück. Daher ist es möglich, dass die Musik, die nach diesem Zeitpunkt für Tasteninstrumente geschrieben wurde, nicht mehr für das Cembalo, sondern für dieses Instrument bestimmt war. Bach war ein gefragter Lehrer, und zu seinen Schülern zählten der zukünftige Mozart-Spezialist und Thomaskantor August Eberhard Müller (s. Schott *Classical Piano Anthology* Bd. 1).

Ludwig van Beethoven (1770–1827)

Beethovens Einfluss auf die musikalische Richtung seiner Zeit sowie auf die musikalische Entwicklung nachfolgender Komponisten war beträchtlich und vielschichtig. Seine eigene stilistische Entwicklung als Komponist lässt sich in drei verschiedene Zeitabschnitte einteilen: bis ca. 1802 (erste Schaffensperiode), von 1802 bis 1812 (zweite Schaffensperiode) und ab 1812 (dritte Schaffensperiode). Hinsichtlich Beethovens Klavierkompositionen reflektieren diese Perioden das klassische Erbe seiner Anfangsphase, die Entwicklung seines virtuosen Spielstils und die darauf folgende Individualität seiner späteren Werke in Bezug auf Technik und Aufbau.

Als Komponist zeichnete sich Beethoven in fast allen Formen der Instrumentalmusik aus, von Streichquartetten über Klaviersonaten und Konzerte bis zu Sinfonien. Die Spontaneität, Stärke und emotionale Wirkung seiner Musik waren jedoch das Ergebnis eines akribisch gestalteten Kompositionsprozesses, den er in seinen Skizzenbüchern und Autographen dokumentierte. Beethoven war ein erfolgreicher Pianist, obgleich seine Leistung in zeitgenössischen Berichten je nach Schwerpunkt des Autors unterschiedlich bewertet wurde. Während einige Beethovens kraftvollen Klang lobten, fanden andere sein Spiel chaotisch und unkontrolliert. Die meisten Quellen sind sich jedoch über die Wirkung einig, die Beethoven mit seinem Spiel auf sein Publikum ausübte.

Ein Klavierwerk, das beide Sichtweisen seines Spiels vereint, ist die Fantasie für Klavier op. 77, ein Werk, das weithin als niedergeschriebene Version einer Improvisation angesehen wird. Es enthält viele für Beethoven typische Aspekte hinsichtlich Harmonik, Melodie und Aufbau und bietet daher einen einzigartigen Einblick in das Schaffen des großen Musikers.

Beethovens kompositorische Leistungen waren so beachtlich, dass nachfolgende Komponistengenerationen von Schubert bis Schumann, Liszt und Brahms einige Zeit zögerten, bevor sie in einem Genre komponierten, das Beethoven sich zuvor zu eigen gemacht hatte.

Domenico Cimarosa (1749–1801)

Cimarosa ist als überaus erfolgreicher Opernkomponist bekannt. Nach seiner Ausbildung als Sänger, Violinist und Pianist in seiner Geburtsstadt Neapel konnte er aufgrund der zunehmenden Beliebtheit seiner Opern von Neapel nach Venedig ziehen, ging anschließend an den russischen Hof in Sankt Petersburg, wo er von 1787–1791 arbeitete, und von dort aus nach Wien, bevor er 1793 nach Neapel zurückkehrte. Seine pro-republikanischen Ansichten brachten ihm im politisch unbeständigen Italien der 1790er-Jahre Schwierigkeiten ein, und nach einem kurzen Gefängnisaufenthalt 1799 kehrte er nach Venedig zurück, wo er 1801 starb.

Cimarosas Bühnenwerke wurden von vielen seiner Zeitgenossen überaus hoch geschätzt. So dirigierte z.B. Haydn einige von Cimarosas Opern. Über die Rezeption seiner Klavierwerke ist hingegen weit weniger bekannt. Die meisten seiner Klaviersonaten sind einsätzig, viele sind zweiteilig. Ihre Transparenz in Verbindung mit dem schematischen Aufbau erinnert an Scarlattis Cembalosonaten, obgleich ihre Melodien typisch für die Klassik sind.

Muzio Clementi (1752–1832)

Clementi wurde in Rom geboren, ging jedoch auf Veranlassung von Peter Beckford (1740–92) 1766 nach England und verbrachte die nächsten sieben Jahre auf dessen Landsitz in Dorset. 1774 übersiedelte Clementi nach London und brach 1780 zu einer europäischen Konzertreise auf. 1782 kritisierte Mozart Clementi in einem Brief an seinen Vater als zu mechanisch, obwohl er dessen Gewandtheit im Spielen von Terzen bewunderte. 1785 war Clementi wieder in London, wo er bis 1802 blieb und nicht nur als Lehrer und Pianist, sondern auch als Verleger, Dirigent und Klavierbauer tätig war. Clementis Leben bestand weiterhin aus diversen musikalischen Aktivitäten (einschließlich Auslandstourneen), obwohl seine geschäftlichen Verantwortungsbereiche immer mehr Zeit in Anspruch nahmen. 1830 setzte er sich zur Ruhe.

Clementi unterrichtete eine Vielzahl erfolgreicher Pianisten und Komponisten, darunter Johann Baptist Cramer, John Field und Friedrich (Frederic) Kalkbrenner. Sein Wissen und sein Beitrag zur Entwicklung des Klavierspiels kommen in seinen zwei wichtigsten Publikationen, *Introduction to the Art of Playing on the Piano Forte* (Lehrbuch)und *Gradus at Parnassum*, einer Sammlung mit Stücken für fortgeschrittene Pianisten, zur Geltung.

Johann Baptist Cramer (1771–1858)

Cramer wurde in Deutschland geboren und zog im Alter von drei Jahren mit seiner Familie nach England. 1783 nahm er ein Jahr lang Unterricht bei Muzio Clementi, dessen Klavierstil Cramer in der Entwicklung seines eigenen Stils prägte. Cramer war bei seinen Kollegen und seinem Publikum für seinen Legato Anschlag bekannt. Wie Clementi zuvor schaffte es Cramer, eine Karriere als Pianist, Lehrer und musikalischer Unternehmer zu kombinieren und war ab 1805 auch als Musikverleger tätig. Diese scheinbar so unterschiedlichen Rollen waren bei den Musikern der zweiten Hälfte des 18. Jahrhunderts durchaus üblich, vor allem, da insbesondere das Verfassen und Veröffentlichen von Unterrichtsmaterial einen lukrativen Markt darstellte. Cramers *84 Etüden* für Klavier (1804 und 1810 in zwei Teilen à 42 Etüden erschienen), die sich an ein breites Publikum richteten, waren sowohl kommerziell erfolgreich als auch ausgesprochen einflussreich, was klavierspielerische Aspekte anging. Beethoven empfahl sie zur Entwicklung der Klavierspieltechnik (er kommentierte ausgewählte Cramer-Etüden und hob deren jeweilige musikalische Ziele hervor), Schumann verwendete sie, Henselt komponierte eine zweite Klavierstimme dazu, und der Liszt-Schüler Carl Tausig (einer der meistgefeierten Pianisten des 19. Jahrhunderts) gab eine Auswahl von Cramer-Etüden heraus und unterstrich somit ein halbes Jahrhundert nach deren Erstveröffentlichung ihre Bedeutung.

Cramers Leben vor 1800 bestand hauptsächlich aus Klavierunterricht und Konzertreisen durch ganz Europa. Nach 1800 hielt er sich hauptsächlich in England auf und konzentrierte sich auf seinen Verlag und das Komponieren. Cramer setzte sich 1835 als hoch angesehenes Mitglied der Londoner Musikszene zur Ruhe.

Carl Czerny (1791–1857)
Czerny hat maßgeblich zur Entwicklung des Klavierspiels beigetragen. Obwohl er hauptsächlich als Beethovens Schüler und Liszts Lehrer bekannt ist, war Czerny ein interessanter eigenständiger Komponist. Die Systematik, mit der er seine eigenen Sammlungen mit Klavierübungen zusammenstellte, entsprach seiner Art, seinen Unterricht bei Beethoven und seine frühen Eindrücke von Liszt gewissenhaft aufzuzeichnen. Kein Wunder, dass er hauptsächlich in diesem Zusammenhang Erwähnung findet.

Czernys Fähigkeiten als Komponist kommen wahrscheinlich am besten in zweien seiner frühen Werke zum Ausdruck: der Klaviersonate op. 7 (1830 von Liszt in Paris gespielt) und seiner hochdramatischen Sinfonie in c-Moll. Mit 16 Jahren entschied sich Czerny gegen eine Laufbahn als Pianist und für den Lehrerberuf. Als Lehrer arbeitete er häufig zehn Stunden und mehr am Tag, bis er sich 1836 zur Ruhe setzte.

Czerny hinterließ das wohl umfassendste Unterrichtsrepertoire aller Klavierlehrer seiner Zeit, wie an seiner *Pianoforte-Schule* op. 500, einem Werk, das er 1846 aktualisierte, zu sehen ist.

Carl Ditters von Dittersdorf (1739–1799)
Dittersdorf war ein österreichischer Violinist und Komponist, der heute hauptsächlich für seine Instrumentalwerke bekannt ist, die nicht für Klavier geschrieben wurden. Zu seinen zahlreichen Werken zählen Oratorien, Sinfonien, Kammermusik und fast alle anderen Genres, mit denen er in Berührung kam. Dies lag höchstwahrscheinlich an seiner Standespflicht als Kapellmeister und Theaterdirektor. Dittersdorf spielte 1763 mit Gluck auf einer Tournee durch Italien Violine, bevor er vom Bischof von Großwardein als Nachfolger von Michael Haydn (Bruder von Joseph Haydn) zum Kapellmeister ernannt wurde. Nach einer Zeit politischer Wirren in den 1770er-Jahren feierte Dittersdorf in der zweiten Hälfte der 1780er-Jahre erneut Erfolge in Wien. Zu dieser Zeit reiste er außerdem nach Berlin, um dort seine Werke aufzuführen.

Dittersdorfs Musik erfreute sich überaus großer Beliebtheit, und auch heute können ihm einige Werke immer noch nicht eindeutig zugeordnet werden.

Johann Wilhelm Häßler (1747–1822)
Häßler wurde 1747 in Erfurt geboren und erhielt von seinem Onkel, dem Erfurter Organisten Johann Christian Kittel, eine musikalische Ausbildung. Im Alter von 16 Jahren spielte Häßler zum ersten Mal als Organist in Erfurt, unternahm jedoch schon bald darauf Konzertreisen durch Deutschland. 1780 gründete er einen eigenen Musikverlag und reiste bis 1790 u. a. nach England und Russland, wo er 1792 Hofkapellmeister in St. Petersburg wurde. In einem Brief von 1788 erinnert sich der Dichter und Schriftsteller Friedrich von Schiller an Häßlers Klavierspiel: „Er spielte meisterhaft. Er komponiert selbst sehr gut. Der Mensch hat viel Originelles und überaus viel Feuer". [1]

Ab 1794 lebte Häßler in Moskau, wo er als hoch angesehener und gefragter Klavierlehrer arbeitete. Sein Beitrag zur Entwicklung des russischen Klavierspiels in der ersten Hälfte des 19. Jahrhunderts ist zwar noch nicht ganz klar, doch geben die meisten seiner veröffentlichten Werke für Klavier Aufschluss darüber, dass er sich auf die Entwicklung der Fähigkeiten weniger erfahrener Pianisten konzentrierte.

Häßler entwickelte seinen eigenen Klavierstil nach dem Vorbild der Klavierwerke von C. P. E. Bach, doch waren seine Werke ebenso zugänglich wie Haydns frühe Klaviersonaten. Viele von Häßlers kürzeren Unterrichtsstücken und leichten Klaviersonaten profitieren von ihrer unmittelbaren musikalischen Anziehungskraft, und seine Klavierschule enthält zahlreiche Werke, die auch heute noch Verwendung finden.

Joseph Haydn (1732–1809)
Die Bewertung von Haydns Stellung als Komponist hat sich im Laufe der Zeit immer wieder verändert. Zahlreiche Berichte konzentrieren sich auf die Sicherheit und Stabilität seiner fast 30-jährigen Anstellung bei der Familie Esterhazy in Eisenstadt bei Wien. Trotz dieses verhältnismäßig beständigen Lebens (zumindest im Vergleich zu vielen seiner Zeitgenossen, nicht zuletzt Mozart) wurde Haydns Musik ab 1780 veröffentlicht und erfreute sich zunehmender Beliebtheit, was dem Komponisten wachsende nationale und internationale Bedeutung einbrachte.

Seine Besuche in London ab 1791 untermauerten seine musikalischen und wirtschaftlichen Erfolge. Seine frühen Jahre sahen jedoch völlig anders aus. Nach seiner Ausbildung als Chorsänger und Violinist hielt sich Haydn, der kein virtuoser Musiker war, mit Unterricht und als Mitglied wechselnder Ensembles, die bei Veranstaltungen musizierten, über Wasser. Als Komponist eignete sich Haydn als Autodidakt nur langsam die notwendigen Fähigkeiten an. Ab Mitte der 1760er-Jahre entwickelte er dann allmählich seinen eigenen Musikstil.

Haydns Klavierwerke umfassen 60 Sonaten, Einzelstücke und Variationen. Obwohl er kein Klaviervirtuose war, wusste er genau, worauf es bei einer Komposition für das Pianoforte ankam. All seine Werke lassen sich sehr gut spielen (ungeachtet ihrer verschiedenen Schwierigkeitsgrade), doch ist das Überraschungsmoment, das sich sowohl in der Harmonik als auch im Aufbau ausdrücken kann, letztendlich für den besonderen Charme vieler Stücke verantwortlich. Haydns Klavierkompositionen sind niemals starr und daher immer unvorhersehbar.

James Hook (1746–1827)
Hooks musikalisches Talent kam schon früh zum Vorschein. Im Alter von sechs Jahren gab er bereits Konzerte und schrieb mit acht Jahren seine ersten größeren Werke, die jedoch heute als verschollen gelten.

Nach seinem Umzug nach London im Jahr 1764 hatte Hook eine Reihe von Stellen als Organist im Raum London, komponierte Vokalmusik, u.a. Opern, und erteilte als gefragter Klavierlehrer Privatunterricht. Seine Tätigkeit als Lehrer erklärt seine zahlreichen didaktischen Werke für Tasteninstrumente, die sowohl elegant als auch technisch anspruchsvoll sind. Die Sonatinen op. 12 wurden 1775 veröffentlicht.

Johann Nepomuk Hummel (1778–1837)
Der Mozartschüler Hummel war zu Lebzeiten eine Schlüsselfigur. Seine Musik blieb sowohl hinsichtlich ihres Aufbaus als auch der musikalischen Details immer ihren klassischen Wurzeln treu. Als Pianist und, was vielleicht am wichtigsten ist, als einflussreicher Klavierlehrer, bildete Hummel jedoch viele Vertreter der ersten Pianistengeneration des 19. Jahrhunderts aus: Henselt, Hiller, Mendelssohn und Thalberg profitierten von Hummels Unterricht.

1) Kahl, W., *Selbstbiographien Deutscher Musiker* (Koeln und Krefeld, Staufen Verlag, 1948), p. 47

Andere Pianisten jeder Zeit wurden ebenfalls von Hummel beeinflusst. Schumann überlegte, bei ihm Unterricht zu nehmen (tat es jedoch nicht), doch beschäftigte er sich mit Hummels Verzierungen für die rechte Hand, wie die *Abegg Variationen* op. 1 und andere Frühwerke belegen. Auch Liszt kam mit Hummels Musik in Berührung, indem er als junger Klaviervirtuose und Konzertreisender dessen Klavierkonzerte op. 85 und 89 spielte. Selbst Chopin muss Hummels Werke gekannt haben, da einige seiner frühen Stücke stilistische, teilweise sogar melodische Ähnlichkeiten aufweisen. Eine von Hummels herausragenden Leistungen ist seine Klavierschule von 1828, ein über 450 Seiten starkes Werk, das den Anspruch hat, den Schüler „vom ersten Unterricht an bis zur vollständigsten Ausbildung" zu begleiten. [1] Es erschien bei Tobias Haslinger (s. Stück Nr. 10 dieser Anthologie) in Wien und ist wahrscheinlich die erste umfassende Klavierschule des 19. Jahrhunderts, in der die technischen Konzepte enthalten sind, die als Grundlagen für das virtuose Klavierspiel jenes Jahrhunderts dienten. Abgesehen von Hummels gründlicher Unterrichtsmethode zeichnet sich die Klavierschule vor allem durch Hummels pädagogische Erkenntnisse und Betrachtungsweisen aus: Interaktion zwischen Schüler und Lehrer, Motivation sowie die Gestaltung einer Unterrichtsstunde sind einige der Themen, mit denen sich Hummel befasste.

Wolfgang Amadeus Mozart (1756–1791)

Mozart wurde in eine äußerst musikalische Familie hineingeboren. Sein Vater Leopold war Orchesterviolinist und Lehrer in Salzburg, und seine ältere Schwester Nannerl hatte bereits ihre Fähigkeiten als Pianistin unter Beweis gestellt. Mozart machte im Musikunterricht rasche Fortschritte – so rasch, dass sein Vater ihn zu einer Konzertreise durch Deutschland und anschließend nach London und Paris mitnahm, die dreieinhalb Jahre dauerte. Danach ließ sich Mozart 1766 in Salzburg nieder. Von 1769–1772 folgten alljährliche Reisen nach Italien, auf denen Mozart – wie in seinem gesamten Leben – Kontakt zu vielen anderen Musikern knüpfte. Anfang der 1780er-Jahre schien Mozart sich in ein Leben als freischaffender Musiker in all seiner Vielfalt eingefunden zu haben. Einige seiner erfolgreichsten Klavierkonzerte stammen aus dieser Zeit, ebenso viele Streichquartette, von denen er einige an der Seite ihres Widmungsträgers, Joseph Haydn, spielte. Am Ende des Jahrzehnts (und zu Beginn des nächsten) feierte Mozart mit Werken wie *Cosi fan tutte* und *Die Zauberflöte* große Erfolge als Opernkomponist.

Die verschiedenen Lebensabschnitte des Komponisten spiegeln sich in der Vielseitigkeit seiner Klavierkompositionen wider. Einige seiner frühesten Werke entstanden, als Mozart erst fünf Jahre alt war, eine Zeit, in der er hauptsächlich kürzere Tänze schrieb. Zu seinen Werken als Erwachsener zählen Sonaten, Variationen und Einzelstücke – viele davon waren für den Eigengebrauch geschrieben.

Ferdinand Ries (1784–1838)

Ries erhielt zunächst von seinem Vater Franz Ries Klavier- und Geigenunterricht. 1801 arbeitete Ries als Notenkopist in München, um seine weitere Ausbildung zu finanzieren, bevor er ein Jahr später nach Wien ging. Dort war er drei Jahre lang Klavierschüler von Beethoven und studierte bei Albrechtsberger Komposition. Beethoven war Ries eine große Starthilfe für seine Karriere als reisender Virtuose, und so trat Ries in den folgenden Jahrzehnten in ganz Europa auf. 1813 kam er nach London und blieb 14 Jahre in England. 1814 heiratete er eine Engländerin. Ries' Zeit in England war wohl die beständigste und finanziell sicherste Zeit seines Lebens. 1824 setzte er sich zur Ruhe und kehrte nach Deutschland zurück – zuerst nach Godesberg und drei Jahre später nach Frankfurt.

Ries' bewahrte in all seinen Werken seine klassischen Wurzeln. Sein erfolgreichstes Klavierwerk war sein Klavierkonzert in cis-Moll op. 55.

Franz Schubert (1797–1828)

Schuberts wurde zunächst von seinem Vater und seinen Brüdern unterrichtet, die ihm Klavier, Violine und Viola beibrachten. Im Alter von elf Jahren erhielt er ein Chorstipendium, das ihm eine Ausbildung bei Salieri ermöglichte. Mit 16 Jahren entschied sich Schubert für eine Ausbildung als Lehrer und begann ein Jahr später, in der Schule seines Vaters zu arbeiten. Mit 17 schrieb er bereits einige seiner frühen Meisterwerke für Klavier und Gesang, den *Erlkönig* und *Gretchen am Spinnrade*. 1816 gab Schubert seinen Lehrerposten auf und ging nach Wien, wo er im Stadtzentrum lebte und sich auf das Komponieren konzentrierte. Eine Zeit der finanziellen Unsicherheit folgte, bis er Ende 1819 sein erstes größeres Kammermusikstück, das *Forellenquintett*, schrieb. Im Frühjahr 1821 führte der Erfolg des *Erlkönigs* zur Veröffentlichung seiner Lieder durch Diabelli, was ihm eine kurze Zeit der finanziellen Sicherheit einbrachte. Von 1820–23 beschäftigte er sich vorwiegend mit der Komposition von Opernmusik, einem nicht besonders erfolgreichen Unterfangen. In seinen drei letzten Lebensjahren widmete er sich der Komposition von Kammermusik und sinfonischen Werken.

Mit wenigen Ausnahmen legte Schubert in seinen Klavierkompositionen nicht so viel Wert auf die äußerlichen technischen Aspekte, die einige seiner Zeitgenossen anwandten. Stattdessen liegen die Herausforderungen seiner Stücke immer in der Musik selbst und dem Bevorzugen von musikalischer Aussage zu rein technischer Darstellung.

Georg Christoph Wagenseil (1715–1777)

Wagenseils historische Bedeutung basiert auf seinem Schaffen als Komponist und Lehrer am österreichischen Hof. In seiner Eigenschaft als Allroundmusiker beeinflusste er die jüngere Komponistengeneration, darunter J. A. Steffan (s. Schott *Classical Piano Anthology* Bd. 3) und F. X. Duschek, und war daher maßgeblich an der Entwicklung des klassischen Stils nach 1750 beteiligt. Seine vier Klavierdivertimenti op. 1–4 erschienen zwischen 1753 und 1763 und waren sofort erfolgreich. Der sechsjährige Mozart spielte bei einem Auftritt 1762 eins von Wagenseils Konzerten, was auf den damaligen Status des Komponisten hindeutet. Kein Wunder, dass es einige Ähnlichkeiten zwischen Wagenseils Klavierkompositionen und Mozarts frühen Notizbüchern gibt. Und doch war Wagenseils Stil mehr als nur ein Sprungbrett zur Klassik. Seine Musik verdankt ihre Eleganz seiner Fähigkeit, hervorragende Unterrichtsstücke zu schreiben, was 1749 zu seiner Ernennung zum Hofklaviermeister führte.

Carl Maria von Weber (1786–1826)

Webers frühe Jahre sind typisch für viele Musiker seiner Zeit. Er erhielt seinen ersten Musikunterricht von seinem Vater und mehreren anderen Musikern. Durch seine Reisen durch Deutschland und Österreich kam Weber in Kontakt mit Michael Haydn (Joseph Haydns Bruder und selbst ein viel beachteter Komponist) sowie dem Komponisten und Musiktheoretiker Georg Joseph Vogler,

---

1) Hummel, J. N., *Anweisung zum Piano-forte spielen* (Wien: Haslinger, 1828)

der Weber den konsequenten Unterricht erteilte, den dieser brauchte. Bis 1810 zog Weber häufig um und übte eine Reihe von musikalischen und teilweise auch Verwaltungstätigkeiten aus. Ein Gerichtsverfahren gegen Weber und seinen Vater, im Zuge dessen beide verhaftet wurden und schließlich Württemberg verlassen mussten, hatte tiefgreifende Auswirkungen auf Weber. Entschlossen, sein Leben zu ändern, verbrachte er die nächsten zwei Jahre damit zu komponieren, Konzerte zu geben und nicht über seine Verhältnisse zu leben. Schon bald folgte eine Ernennung zum Hof- und/oder Theaterdirigenten, von 1813 bis 1816 in Prag und von 1817 bis 1821 in Dresden. In dieser Zeit unternahm er außerdem Konzertreisen. Für die wohl bedeutendste Veränderung in Webers Leben war die große Beliebtheit seiner Oper *Der Freischütz* (1820) verantwortlich, ein Werk, das ihm sowohl in Deutschland als auch international Erfolg einbrachte.

Webers Klavierstücke sind zwar sehr charakteristisch, jedoch schwer zu beschreiben. Sie sind eindeutig melodieorientiert wie viele von Webers mehrstimmigen Kompositionen. Ein besonderer Schwerpunkt liegt auf Tanzformen und punktierten Rhythmen, die seinen Musikstil unterstreichen. Als Pianist bevorzugte Weber raffinierte und oft virtuose Passagen für die rechte Hand, schnelle Akkordfolgen, Überkreuzen der Hände und Sprünge, die weit über eine Fünf-Finger-Position hinausgehen. In diesem Sinne beruhen Webers Klavierkompositionen auf der fließenden Tonleiter- und Arpeggiotechnik, die Hummel bevorzugte, nehmen jedoch eine Mittelstellung zwischen Hummel und dem von Chopin und Liszt geforderten Klavierspiel ab 1830 ein.

Samuel Wesley (1766–1837)

Samuel Wesley war eine brillante, jedoch teilweise umstrittene Persönlichkeit des damaligen Musiklebens. Er wurde in Bristol geboren und zog 1771 mit seinen Eltern nach London, wo Wesley im Haus der Familie in Marylebone sein musikalisches Können schon früh in Auftritten unter Beweis stellte. William Boyce bezeichnete den jungen Musiker 1774 als „englischen Mozart" – ein Hinweis auf Wesleys frühen Erfolg. Wesley war zwar eigentlich Organist, doch sind seine musikalischen Aktivitäten typisch für die Musiker seiner Zeit. Er verdiente seinen Lebensunterhalt mit einer Mischung aus Privatunterricht, Konzertauftritten und Kompositionen. Obwohl er als Musiker großes Ansehen genoss, verhinderten sein unkonventionelles Privatleben und seine häufigen Depressionen, dass er im Zentrum des englischen Musiklebens stand. Leider ist heute ein Großteil seiner Klaviermusik trotz ihres leicht zugänglichen Stils und ihrer innovativen Frische nicht mehr erhältlich.

Nils Franke

Bibliografie

Hinson, Maurice.
Guide to the Pianist's Repertoire.
Bloomington and Indianapolis: Indiana University Press, 2000

MacGrath, Jane.
The Pianist's Guide to Standard Teaching and Performance Literature.
Van Nuys: Alfred Publishing Co., 1995

Prosnitz, Adolf.
Handbuch der Klavierliteratur.
Wien: Doblinger, 1908

Sadie, Stanley (ed.)
Grove Concise Dictionary of Music.
London: MacMillan Publishers, 1988

Sadie, Stanley (ed.)
Grove Dictionary of Music online.
[accessed 04/04/2011]

Wolters, Klaus.
Handbuch der Klavierliteratur zu zwei Händen.
Zürich and Mainz: Atlantis Musikbuch Verlag, 2001

Romantic Piano Anthology

Original Works from the Romantic period
Selected and edited by Nils Franke

- Both mainstream and lesser-known works from composers such as Chopin, Schumann, Gounod and Rimsky-Korsakov

- Graded pieces new to the graded framework presented in a progressive order

- Extensive commentary on each piece

- Composer biographies included

- CD recording of all the pieces played by Nils Franke

Volume 1 (Grades 1-2) ED 12912	**Volume 2** (Grades 3-4) ED 12913
Volume 3 (Grades 5-6) ED 12914	**Volume 4** (Grades 7-8) ED 12915

"This is a lovely book reflecting Schott's renowned high standards and interest in piano pedagogy."

Romantic Piano Anthology 2 - **Music Teacher Magazine**

SCHOTT

Improvising Blues Piano

by Tim Richards

ED 12504

Improvising Blues Piano examines the harmonic, rhythmic and melodic aspects of the blues. All styles are covered from the 1920s to the present, from the early boogie pioneers via swing, gospel, jump-jive, New Orleans, Chicago and Kansas City schools, to the more sophisticated jazz and funky blues of the current scene.

" ...the essential book for all aspiring blues pianists."
Jools Holland

"This book leaves any possible competition standing at the post."
Brian Priestley, Jazzwise

Exploring Jazz Piano

by Tim Richards

Vol. 1 ED 12708 | Vol 2 ED 12829

BEST POP PUBLICATION

Winner of the 2006 **MIA Award** for *Best Pop Publication*

The long-awaited follow-up to Tim Richards' acclaimed *Improvising Blues Piano*, fills a vacuum in jazz piano instruction. Any jazz piano student, piano teacher, or performing musician dipping into either volume will be rewarded with a wealth of ideas and practical information to keep them occupied for many months, or to use as an ongoing resource in the years to come.

"...demands to be in the library of every Music Department that teaches jazz."
Hugh Johns, Times Educational Supplement

"I cannot praise it too highly... Vol. 1 and 2 together rank among the best instructional books that I have seen in the 21 years since Jazzwise started."
Charles Alexander, Jazzwise

Discovering Rock Piano

by Jürgen Moser

Vol. 1 ED 13069 | Vol. 2 ED 13070

Whether you're a budding rock keyboardist or classically-trained pianist looking to develop your performance skills in other genres, *Discovering Rock Piano* reveals all the secrets of how to play today's rock and pop music on piano or keyboard.

Chord playing, rhythmic confidence and instructions for improvisation with systematic exercises and songs form the focus of the first volume while the second volume presents all the possible techniques for playing rock piano from which you can develop your own individual style.

Exploring Latin Piano

by Tim Richards and John Crawford

ED 13216

A unique collaboration between two of the the UK's top pianist/educators, John Crawford de Cominges and Tim Richards.

A detailed introduction to the highly rhythmic music of Latin America and Spain, featuring over 50 pieces in a wide range of styles from many countries including the mambo from Cuba, the samba from Brazil, the tango from Angentina and the flamenco from Spain.

CD Track List / Plages du CD / CD-Titelverzeichnis

No.	Title	Composer	Duration
1.	Allegro, from Divertimento No. 2 WWV43	Georg Christoph Wagenseil	1:17
2.	Sonata in G major	Domenico Cimarosa	1:25
3.	Rondo, from Sonatina Op. 12 No. 9	James Hook	1:02
4.	English Dance No. 15	Carl Ditters von Dittersdorf	1:28
5.	Guaracha, from Pianoforte Method	Johann Baptist Cramer	0:34
6.	Vivace, from Sonatina Op. 12 No. 8	Samuel Wesley	1:09
7.	Allegro, from Pianoforte Method	Johann Nepomuk Hummel	0:51
8.	Ländler D378 No. 3	Franz Schubert	0:43
9.	Ländlerischer Tanz WoO 11 No. 2	Ludwig van Beethoven	0:45
10.	Praeludium and Andantino, from Pianoforte Method	Johann Baptist Cramer	1:01
11.	Allegro assai Op. 38 No. 20	Johann Wilhelm Hässler	0:49
12.	Presto Op. 38 No. 29	Johann Wilhelm Hässler	0:26
13.	Andante Op. 453 No. 32	Carl Czerny	1:02
14.	Scherzo, from Sonata Hob. XVI:9	Joseph Haydn	0:58
15.	Solfeggio, from Musikalische Nebenstunden	Johann Christoph. F. Bach	0:49
16.	Tempo di Minuetto KV236	Wolfgang Amadeus Mozart	1:39
17.	Arietta, from Pianoforte Method	Muzio Clementi	1:23
18.	Polonaise Op. 124 No. 3	Ferdinand Ries	1:25
19.	Andantino Op. 453 No. 41	Carl Czerny	1:32
20.	Romanze Op. 52 No. 4	Johann Nepomuk Hummel	1:32
21.	Gigue, from Pianoforte Method	Johann Nepomuk Hummel	0:46
22.	Favoritwaltzer J. 143–8 No. 4	Carl Maria von Weber	2:45
23.	Favoritwaltzer J. 143–8 No. 2	Carl Maria von Weber	1:48
24.	Adagio Hob. XVII:9	Joseph Haydn	4:12
25.	Klavierstück, *Lustig-Traurig* WoO 54	Ludwig van Beethoven	2:12
	Total duration		**33:21**